Elizaveta Gaufman and Bharath Ganesh
The Trump Carnival

De Gruyter Contemporary Social Sciences

Volume 35

Elizaveta Gaufman and Bharath Ganesh

The Trump Carnival

—

Populism, Transgression and the Far Right

DE GRUYTER

This book has been published open access thanks to the financial support of the Open Access Book Fund of the University of Groningen.

ISBN 978-3-11-221617-0
e-ISBN (PDF) 978-3-11-123813-5
e-ISBN (EPUB) 978-3-11-124229-3
ISSN 2747-5689
e-ISSN 2747-5697
DOI https://doi.org/10.1515/9783111238135

Library of Congress Control Number: 2023946745

Bibliographic information published by the Deutsche Nationalbibliothek
The Deutsche Nationalbibliothek lists this publication in the Deutsche Nationalbibliografie; detailed bibliographic data are available on the Internet at http://dnb.dnb.de.

© 2025 with the author(s), published by Walter de Gruyter GmbH, Berlin/Boston. This book is published with open access at www.degruyter.com.
This volume is text- and page-identical with the hardback published in 2024.
Cover image: Elizaveta Gaufman / DALLE
Printing and binding: CPI books GmbH, Leck

www.degruyter.com

Contents

Chapter 1: Introduction

"Fuck the blue!"
"Our house!"
"Let the people in!"
"Hang 'em!"
"Bring Nancy Pelosi out here now. We want to hang that fucking bitch. Bring her out!"

These are just some of the exclamations heard during the storming of the Capitol Building in Washington DC in the US on January 6, 2021. Disgruntled Trump supporters, egged on during the Stop the Steal rally by Trump himself and his associates, stormed and breached the Capitol Building, forcing the Congressional proceedings of election certification to be suspended and members of Congress to flee the building. The mob of violent insurrectionists, shrieking incoherencies, made their way to the congressional offices and chambers. Vice President Mike Pence was supposed to be presiding over the certification and, having declined President Trump's illicit request to thwart the certification, declared Joe Biden the President-elect. He too was evacuated from the building and rightly so: the crowd was heard chanting "hang Mike Pence" and even erected a gallows outside. The insurrectionists left behind a trail of destruction, violence, and excrement, with five people losing their lives during the attack.

For most Americans, some of whom might trace a previous Capitol Building storming back to the war with the British in 1812, it was probably very traumatic to watch the footage of the insurrection. For those who did the storming or supported it, the same event was the climax of their idea to take back control from those they considered to be the corrupt elite who stole 'their' election; the same elite that conspiracy myth-mongers portrayed as a bloodthirsty cabal of pedophiles (with space lasers) bent on destroying an idealized vision of the United States. While the January 6 committee as well as numerous media outlets have highlighted this transgression of the tradition of American politics, the insurrection was indicative of the change in the way politics works in the United States. While right-wing personalities tried to defend the insurrectionists by highlighting their adherence to the norms ("they were walking along the velvet ropes!"), the events on January 6 have shown that those norms had been broken long before that day. In fact, the whole idea of transgressing democratic norms has been the rallying cry of Trump supporters from day one.

"The sensitive ear will always catch even the most distant echoes of a carnival sense of the world," wrote literary philosopher Mikhail Bakhtin in his book on Dostoyevsky. In the case of the January 6 insurrection, the echoes were not distant at all: the ritual abuse, the profanities, even the feces smeared inside Congress are very much emblematic of the carnival culture that describes the transgression of cultural norms and values by 'the people.' Even though Donald Trump, as a rich, white, straight male can hardly be seen as a marginalized voice, he nevertheless managed to galvanize a substantial amount of support among the American population by marketing himself as an anti-establishment figure, i.e., a voice of the 'regular' people, by using elements of carnival culture. Charles Lock complained that many scholars selectively read Bakhtin and make him into a linguist, a semiotician, a deviant Formalist, a revisionist Marxist, a theorist of fiction, a categorist of genres (Lock 1991). Well, we are making Mikhail Mikhailovich into a political scientist.

What is carnival and why should you care about it in the context of American politics? Let us begin with the second question. For starters, many politicians, pundits, political scientists, and regular people have clutched at their pearls, thrown their hands in the air, or torn their hair out at the spectacle that has been the Trump campaign, the Trump presidency, his second campaign in 2020, and the aftermath of his loss. "Carnival barking clown," "carnival fool," "carnival act," and similar epithets have been thrown around rather consistently and emphatically. In this book, we show that these comparisons were not far from the truth, so let us explain what carnival in this context means. We are not discussing the carnival fairs of today, with rides, tents, and junk food; together with Mikhail Mikhailovich, we are going back to the Renaissance. Back then, a carnival was a period of sanctioned levity, where people in medieval European cities were allowed by the powers that be to engage in activities that the Church frowned upon: for instance you could eat lots of meat (hence "carne" in the name—meat). Carnival liberates carnal desire and encourages transgression, where you can swear as much as you want, disguise yourself, and harass women and minorities. The carnival square is where lots of people talk, touch each other, eat, copulate, and laugh. The carnival ethos stood in opposition to the 'official' and 'serious' Church-sanctioned and feudal culture, by bringing out folklore and different forms of folk laughter that Bakhtin calls carnival. This type of culture challenges the official buttoned-up discourse and is characterized by coarseness and vulgarity, distinguished by its anti-ideology and anti-authority themes. In other words, carnival is anti-establishment, something that the 'blue-collar billionaire' emphasized in almost every rally and speech. This book is not the first attempt to apply Bakhtin's framework to the study of politics, and Donald Trump is not the first 'carnival fool' to succeeded in politics (Bordignon and Ceccarini 2013; Bartlett et al. 2013). However, we take the carnivalesque framework further and show how it explains the normalization of racism, antidemocratic politics, and fascism.

Carnival is not only about fools and laughter, when 'the people' feel like they have the power, things can turn ugly. The storming of the Capitol is often seen as a violent culmination of Trump's populist politics, but Trump was in fact firmly within the right-wing American populist tradition. There is always a degree of populism in a representative democracy (Dulio and Klemanski 2018) and the claim to represent 'common people' or everyday Americans has driven American politics in multiple election cycles in the 19th, 20th, and 21st centuries. Who counted as the common people in the span of American history is, of course, a matter of debate. From Jacksonian voting rights expansion in the 1830s and Huey Long's crusade against the wealthy elite to Sarah Palin's soccer mom-turned-politician agenda, not to mention the populism of the second half of the 20th century (Bonikowski and Gidron 2016), Trump was not necessarily an aberration in the existing political landscape. While scores of articles, academic and journalistic, are written about the populist zeitgeist and the rise of populist politics connected to the election of Donald Trump, former Brazilian president Jair Bolsonaro or the success of the Brexit vote, we would like to emphasize a different aspect of what most scholars call populist politics. Namely, while most academics focus on the juxtaposition of the pure people and the corrupt elite, we focus on the politics of transgression and carnivalesque features.

Where can the appetite for transgression be found? Candidates have often tried to exploit the changes in internal party dynamics to their advantage (Rackaway and Rice 2018). One of the main drivers of this phenomenon was the partisan change in so-called unhyphenated Americans (Arbour 2018), where white Americans who do not identify with their European countries of origin constituted one of the main forces in Trump's support. At the same time, his success in 'Trump country' was just another marginally improved Republican victory among this electorate that was often motivated by the rhetoric of nostalgia (Brownstein 2016) that sought to capitalize on a myth of what America supposedly once was coupled with the crude rhetoric of winning (Mason 2018). As Barone notes, both the Democratic party and the Republican party each maintained a relatively constant character, at least in the second half of the twentieth century, with the former representing a coalition of "out-groups" and the latter appealing to "typical Americans" as understood at a given time (Barone 2019). This distinction is crucial not only for populists, but also for the politics of carnival.

This book should be published in early 2024, during yet another United States presidential campaign in which Donald Trump is running. As we write this book, Trump has been charged in criminal cases in three states: New York, Florida, and Georgia, as well as Washington DC (Politico Staff 2023). At the time of writing, he commands the lead in the 2024 Republican primary with a massive margin over his competitors. When Trump boasted two weeks before the Iowa caucus in 2016 that he could shoot someone and still not lose any voters (Dwyer 2016), almost eight years and 91 felony charges later, the majority of Republican Iowa caucus delegates still support him. His 2016 quip, tragically, seems all too true. As we show, carnival has become an entrenched part of American politics, having broken a number of taboos and making transgression a value. We hope that by reminding readers of the previous two campaigns and the Trump presidency, we can help make sense of the damage done to American democracy since 2015.

* * *

This book's aims are threefold. First, we offer a Bakhtinian analysis of American electoral politics since 2015 that led to the election of Donald Trump. Each chapter is devoted to specific aspects of the carnivalesque culture, emphasizing multidirectional discourse, displaced abjection, laughing culture, misogyny, and sex. Each chapter begins with a more general American Studies perspective on the carnivalesque item in question and then reflects on the way Bakhtin's framework rethinks and reconceptualizes the existing literature. Second, we analyze the way carnivalesque elements have been visible in Trump rallies, the mass media covering them, and the mainstream late-night comedy shows that followed, as well as various social media platforms. Third, we argue that the disruptive nature of carnival signified by Trump's campaign and later politics is one of the causes of the erosion of democratic institutions in the US. And as we are talking about carnival in all its carnal, transgressive glory, this book will feature obscene vocabulary and obscene subjects. Be forewarned.

Chapter 2: Populism and Transgression

Anyone but a social scientist could be forgiven for claiming Donald Trump is a *populist*. This moniker has become one of the most common appellations to describe Trump's brand of politics, hearkening back to segregationist Democrat George Wallace of Alabama, who personally blocked Black students arriving at the University of Alabama after it was forced to integrate (Jamison 2022). The term populist is quite possibly the most effective euphemism of our time, laundering racists and fascists into ostensibly people-centric politicians giving voice to the unheard working class. This narrative is nonsense of course, Trump is about as 'elite' as it gets, even if many leading columnists in the papers became convinced by the 'populist' description after the 2016 election. This narrative is not just nonsense. It is foolish. It prevents us from seeing what Trump, and the others that pundits label 'populists,' clearly are. But it is also the term that dominates public discussion about the resurgent anti-democratic, anti-equality, and anti-pluralist politics that compromise fundamental rights and human dignity. So, if we want to talk about Trump and the erosion of democracy, we cannot avoid discussing populism.

Trump's election in 2016 shattered the expectations of pundits, pollsters, journalists, and scholars alike. His success catapulted the term 'populism'—the focus of debate in what was a relatively marginal subfield of (primarily) European political science—to the forefront of political consciousness across the world. Before we knew it, Trump was not only a populist, he was its *archetype*. Researchers leapt on this term, which lurched from relative obscurity in political science to becoming what is among the fastest-growing keywords in the social sciences. Columnists from periodicals, primarily on the left and center, found it to be the most descriptive term for the rise of Trump and for Brexit. Populism, invoked across Western Europe, became the dragnet expression for rebranded fascists. Considering use of the word 'populism' in the English broadsheet *The Guardian* in expressions such as "populist hype," Brown and Mondon (2021) argue that the newspaper frequently collapses the *far right* into 'populism.' Like Brown and Mondon, we believe that this has serious impacts. They argue that (1) the populist hype protects elites (e.g., leaders of movements, like Trump) from blame for far-right, racist, and extreme discourse, instead blaming it on the (white) 'working class'; that (2) it euphemizes and trivializes racism, such as Islamophobia, as a feature of 'populism' rather than a fundamental feature of far-right politics; and that (3), by focusing on populism, thanks to the 'hype,' ultimately *The Guardian* and other papers inadvertently amplify the far right.

The populist surge, which ostensibly began in 2016, also affects Western Europe (to mention one region among many). Just a few months before Donald

Trump surprised the world by winning the presidential election, a slim margin of British voters delivered Brexit, an idea tabled by the upstart party, UKIP (UK Independence Party). In a now iconic image, Brexiteer-in-Chief, Nigel Farage of UKIP (MEP for South East England at the time), stood in front of a "Vote Leave" poster, featuring the faces of hundreds of ostensible migrants and emblazoned with the words "Breaking Point," claiming the "EU has failed us all." The poster is nonsensical. The migrants pictured mostly appear to be non-European. It was displayed in the context of major inflows of migrants that nationalist parties across Europe used to propel their agenda. Brexit could only stop the migration of Europeans into the UK, and yet today (after disgraced Prime Minister Boris Johnson finalized Brexit), the UK has a record number of immigrants. It is important to remember that Nigel Farage went to a fee-paying school (Rawnsley 2022) while his ancestors ostensibly fled religious prosecution in France. Before Brexit, he had been an MEP for sixteen years. Certainly a career politician, and hardly "working class." Yet after the campaign, Farage was the British face of this 'populist' surge. In France, Marine Le Pen (daughter of Jean-Marie Le Pen, who founded the far-right party Front national, directed a presidential campaign for a Nazi collaborator in 1965, and is a convicted Holocaust denier) revived her father's party in 2011 and has been a strong contender for the French presidency. Today, the party—which has demonstrable roots in French fascism (Ivaldi and Lanzone 2016)—has been renamed Rassemblement National (National Rally). Marine Le Pen, who is no doubt a far-right politican and runs a party founded by fascists, is frequently referred to by pundits and columnists as a populist.

As a final example, take Giorgia Meloni, who in 2022 became the first woman to be elected Prime Minister of Italy. She was active in the youth wing of the fascist political party the Movimento Sociale Italiano (MSI) and praised Mussolini in her teens, before becoming an MP in the conservative Alleanza Nazionale (National Alliance) party that grew out of the defunct MSI. In 2012, she founded the far-right party Fratelli d'Italia and became a prominent politician on the right in Italy, before finding her way to the top job after electoral success and coalition-building in 2022. After her election, Sky News's Europe correspondent Adam Parsons *claimed* that "no, she's not a fascist, a word that gets thrown around far too carelessly" (Parsons 2022). For someone that spent their entire career in Italy's post-fascist parties and maintains well-documented extreme positions across the board, it is hardly careless to call her a fascist. But she's just a social conservative, according to Parsons.

Journalists, pundits, and many others use the term populist to describe the far right, and to a degree, we are stuck with populism if we want to talk about the far right. Political scientists, however, make some compelling points for why we *should* use the term populism to describe politicians like Trump. Political scientists are agnostic about where on the left-right spectrum a populist sits. Populism is discursive and rhetorical, and describes a politician that claims to speak for the 'people' who are (supposedly) ignored by elites. According to the dominant view among political scientists, populism is a 'thin ideology' that is associated with thicker ideologies, such as socialism, environmentalism, nationalism, or fascism. Others argue that it is purely stylistic; that while populists can sit anywhere on the ideological spectrum, it is how they present themselves—by flaunting the 'low' culture versus the 'high' culture of elites—that makes them populist. For the most part, political scientists do not just study 'populism,' but tend to study populism in conjunction with other movements. The parties of Farage, Le Pen, and Meloni are broadly characterized by political scientists as radical right parties. In some cases, political scientists add populism as a qualifier to refer to the *populist radical right.* This qualifier is primarily based on how these actors *enact* politics. Political scientists, for example, see populism in how these actors claim to speak for a 'pure' people, defined as the 'native' population. (This claim is of course absurd in settler colonial contexts like Australia, Canada, and the US, where it is primarily about the maintenance of racial dominance for those constructed as 'white.') Others see populism in Donald Trump's style, for example, in his angry tone and crass manners. This makes him look more 'real', 'authentic', and closer to 'the people' than the well-heeled suits we imagine in Washington DC. This style makes Trump populist, but that matters less than his ideology.

Despite its problems, there is something useful in the term populism. But it is not a term to replace *far right*, which identifies a global family of political parties —well beyond North America and Western Europe—and accurately describes the political movement that is eroding democracy today. It is important to remember that while we focus on Trump, he is not an anomaly. Across the world we find far-right politicians both in power and trying to obtain it. Narendra Modi, Jair Bolsonaro, Viktor Orban, and Benjamin Netanyahu are far-right contemporaries of Trump—like the Western Europeans mentioned above—with rather varying commitments to "populism". Few would refer to Modi and Netanyahu as populists, but they are certainly far-right and appeal to a sense of a pure, ethnically and religiously bound, people. Bolsonaro, on the other hand, enacts a populist style along with extremist politics. As a term, "populism", either as a descriptor of a politician or as an object of study, should have relatively narrow applications. When it is used in the press to describe the far right without a qualifier, it normalizes racism, anti-democratic politics, and fascism.

All the same, there is something curiously populist about Trump and other radical right cultures. This populism is not about style as such, but rather about the collective violation of—quite literally for the insurrectionist that smeared shit on the Capitol—the rules, values, symbols, and institutions of democracy. Fundamentally, what is populist here is its *transgressive* aspect: both its articulation of taboos, ostensibly put in place by an elite, and the encouragment of their violation. When Trump, as we argue in this book, creates the carnival, he creates a space that not only gives license to but encourages violation. But what matters is *what* Trump violates, which also reveals what kind of a populist he is. The Trump carnival is fundamentally anti-democratic; as its carnival fool, Trump's transgressions—taking pride in grabbing pussies and mocking political correctness—are an invitation for others to do the same. The Trump carnival is about the collective violation of democracy itself. It is about taking joy in the violation of claims to equality and representation, by a group of people who mythologize themselves as victims because they no longer have dominance over others. We argue that this transgression and violation of democracy is central to the far right today. By studying the Trump carnival, we make clear how this movement uses play, transgression, laughter, and misogyny to erode democracy while celebrating its downfall.

2.1 Populism

As we discussed previously in relation to Bakhtin's theory of carnival, the focus on popular culture, its folkloric response to 'official' and 'serious' church-sanctioned culture, and its use of laughter and vulgarity are all aspects that make carnival *populist*. In this book, we frame populism differently than most political scientists or journalists. As discussed above, journalistic discussions of populism tend towards its uncritical use as a moniker for the far right. Instead, we focus on carnival to make sense of how Trump makes use of populism. In this section, we briefly introduce theories of populism in political science and in communication studies (which has also picked up the term). In doing so we develop a critique of the term in scientific work to better explain why it is only in the carnival that it makes sense to speak of Trump as a populist. We introduce this idea here, and the following chapters flesh out how the Trump carnival works.

As mentioned above, there are some excellent reasons why populism is a useful term to describe Donald Trump. Political scientists provide two main ones, referred to in debates as the 'ideational' approach to populism and the 'socio-cultural' approach to populism. Others also discuss populism as organizational, but that is beyond the scope of this book. The 'ideational' approach is dominant in the field, and the vast majority of political scientists would place themselves in this camp. However, we find the 'socio-cultural' approach to populism more convincing, which is what we discuss here. Both of these approaches have significant flaws that have not sufficiently been addressed by the field. We do not intend to provide an in-depth or complete review of these ideas here. Rather, we only outline two major positions and explain how our theorization of carnival as an analytical framework for the Trump phenomenon relates to these broader debates.

Populism is useful for scientific purposes: it provides scholars and researchers with a set of formal features that describe political movements that challenge elite power in a multitude of ways across the world, and that do indeed share some features. Researchers—for the most part—tend to conceive of populism as a 'thin' (at best) ideology that is attached to 'thicker' ideologies. In this sense, populism has little ideological content on its own, so it is at best a fuzzy concept. The 'ideational' definition of populism, developed by Cas Mudde, is without doubt the dominant approach to populism in political science. It is best summarized by the following, which is, at this point, an obligatory citation in the field:

> [Populism is] an ideology that considers society to be ultimately separated into two homogeneous and antagonistic groups, 'the pure people' versus 'the corrupt elite,' and which argues that politics should be an expression of the *volonté générale* (general will) of the people. (2004, p. 543)

To Mudde, this implies that there are four elements that we must understand to discuss populism: ideology, the people, the elite, and the general will. Ideology is not-predetermined; while populism, as Mudde argues, includes some ideological content of its own (it constructs the people and the elite and articulates the people's will, whatever that may be), it does not prescribe a grander, thicker theory of a social order, legal principles, or a vision of power as Western ideologies such as liberalism, socialism, and fascism do. In this sense, the ideational approach is agnostic to ideological content. The people are, of course, the center of populism. The 'people' are constructed as a *morally pure* and *righteous* 'idealization' of a community. For Mudde, the moral evaluation of populism is central: if the people are 'pure,' then the 'elite' are fundamentally corrupt. In this sense, populism's construction of the people is not (in theory, here) racial, but instead based on the sense of 'doing the right thing,' which is the opposite of the actions taken by the corrupt elite who are fundamentally out of step with the moral purity of the people. Indeed, it is the elites that *betray* the people. Finally, the idea of the 'general will' contends that the morally pure people speak with only one voice, are fundamentally homogeneous, and that politics should follow only their 'will,' alone and that the populist is their ultimate representative.

Mudde is an expert on the populist radical right, and we should stress that he is very clear in that he is fundamentally concerned about *the far right* and not populism as such (see Mudde 2020). We share this assessment while noting that the features of populism Mudde describes are readily applicable to Trump. Trump indeed claims to speak for an imagined, 'pure' people through what political scientists usually refer to as 'nativist' appeals (at least in comparative research) in which one group of people is constructed as 'native' in that their territory (e.g., the US, France, etc.) is their *birthright*.[1] Ultimately, nativism is fundamentally about constructing *race* in the US and Western Europe: it is about constructing the idea of Western culture facing a civilizational threat (Brubaker 2017). This threat, primarily, comes from the 'liberal elites' whose support of immigrants, refugees, and Muslims (in particular) compromises 'real' Americans and is the root cause of an apparent cultural degeneracy in American cities and culture.

Today, the 'war on woke' is an extension of this idea that cultural elites—such as those working in equality, inclusion and diversity in the corporate sector or intellectuals who discuss the US's violent and racist foundations—seek to compromise everything that 'real' Americans believe. Who are these 'real' Americans? It doesn't take a genius to figure out that 'real' here really means 'white,' and Trump has made almost no effort to distance himself from white supremacist groups. Most of the time, he launders their reputations (reminding us there's "very fine people on both sides" even when one side is chanting, "Jews will not replace us"; see Gray 2017) or encourages them (the Proud Boys ought to "stand back and stand by," until January 6, 2021 at least; see Ronayne and Kunzelman 2020). Fundamentally, Trump articulated an imagined, righteous 'white' community that is being betrayed by a cosmopolitan, liberal establishment. In this manner, Mudde's definition of populism, at least in the abstract, works quite well: we have a 'pure people,' articulated as a *race*, downtrodden by an 'elite' and a leader that claims to speak for them.

As many researchers have found, in the US, the radical right is primarily concerned with the diminished superiority of the withering entitlements and privileges that accrue to 'white' Americans (McVeigh and Estep 2020). Where many argue that populists are representative of the losers of globalization, the reality is that the resentment that many anthropologists and sociologists study is a backlash against the advancement of the equality of racial, religious, and sexual minorities. Here, Toni Morrison's insights are (as ever) piercing; writing in *The New Yorker* in the aftermath of Trump's election, she states:

> The comfort of being 'naturally better than,' of not having to struggle or demand civil treatment, is hard to give up. The confidence that you will not be watched in a department store,

---

1 Application of the term "nativism" to describe Trump is nonsensical; the white identity that he speaks to is of course not native to North America. The appellation is also questionable in Europe, given its long history of migration within and across the continent. Nativism thus involves the *construction* of a community or group of people as native, and has no necessary relation to truth. It is purely a rhetorical device, which is not always clear in political science research.

that you are the preferred customer in high-end restaurants—these social inflections, belonging to whiteness, are greedily relished [...] so scary are the consequences of a collapse of white privilege that many Americans have flocked to a political platform that supports and translates violence against the defenseless as strength. (Morrison 2016)

Anthropologists indeed come to some similar findings. In one of the books that has received the most attention in recent years, *Strangers in Their Own Land*, Arlie Hochschild (2018) paints a rich picture of this sense of lost privilege. In Europe, Norris and Inglehart make a similar observation about what they refer to as "authoritarian populism" as a backlash by conservatives against the increasing diversity and visibility of racial and sexual minorities in Europe, which they enact not for economic reasons but due to cultural anxieties about 'whiteness' in Europe (see 2019, p. 205).

Populism, in Mudde's definition, fits well here, because of the centrality of white identity for the populist radical right in Europe and North America. In references to 'real' Americans and 'the people', the populist radical right primarily refers to white Europeans and Americans. The construction of the 'morally pure' people is not, as may be the case with other forms of populism, about class but about race. The community, the idea of common sense, and the 'general will' all begin from this presupposition. Thus, the attitudes of Norris and Inglehart's "authoritarian populist" become *commonsensical*, such as the idea that European culture is under threat of Islamization (one of Meloni's favored claims on Twitter before she became PM; see Ganesh and Froio 2020) or that 'real' American culture faces degenerate influences such as feminism, Marxism, and multiculturalism. In all cases, it is the 'elites'—Barack Obama, Hillary Clinton, George Soros, and the coastal 'latte-sipping' liberals—that collude with immigrants, feminists, multiculturalists, and progressives to destroy the 'real' American culture. In this narrative, the 'pure people' are those who identify with white America and see their 'way of life' as under threat. Thus, we have the curious but absurd construction of white Americans as the primary victims in contemporary American society.

Our assertions are backed up by a large volume of quantitative research on the US electorate. This is why we opened the chapter with the claim that anyone *but* a social scientist could be forgiven for calling Trump a populist. Social scientists have come to the consensus that not only did Trump's election depend on white voters' anxiety regarding their racial entitlements and privileges—those "social inflections" that Toni Morrison argues are "greedily relished"—but that Trump normalized extreme, white supremacist narratives and rhetoric (Fording and Schram 2020). In an extensive analysis of both official polling data from the 2016 election and historical data, Fording and Schram (2020) argue that not only does "outgroup hostility" include racial animus towards Black Americans, but also that, "in an age of growing concern about globalization, immigration, and multiculturalism, outgroup hostility came to include other racialized groups, especially Latinx immigrants and Muslims" (p. 24). They find that "the effect of outgroup hostility was substantively larger than the effects of any of the other independent variables and actually comparable to the effect of party identification" (p. 163). Repeated exposure to Trump's demonization of refugees, immigrants, and Muslims, according to this research, far outweighed factors such as education in predicting votes for him. And while they find that white identity did not have a direct relation to increasing the vote share for Trump, white identification played an important role in activating this outgroup hostility, as did economic anxieties (pp. 169–170). Fording and Schram also find that outgroup hostility also explains anger towards Democrats and enthusiasm for Republicans in the period 2004–2016, with such hostility increasing sharply after the election of Obama (pp. 180–181). The correlation that Fording and Schram (2020) observe between anger towards Democrats and outgroup hostility is, in their view, evidence that Trump's victory "was a monument to the mainstreaming of racism" (p. 182). Others argue that Christian nationalism and white identity had a significant impact in predicting Trump vote intention, more so than education or income (Whitehead and Perry 2020). Overall, there is precious little data to suggest that economic or class-based explanations were important in the election.

What Fording and Schram (2020) do point out is that emotion, particularly as it is activated by white identity, plays a key role in activating outgroup hostility. While the authors focus on racial resentment as Trump expresses it in his speeches, our theorization of the Trump carnival can build on these findings. As we discuss in the chapter on displaced abjection, expressing hostility towards outgroups is a fundamental aspect of carnival. Here, we are mostly concerned with dispelling the idea that Trump is a simple populist. He is a white supremacist whose electoral success greatly depended on racial conservatives and extremists whose animus towards minorities, immigrants, and Muslims was at the center of their politics. Populism, then, attaches to this much *thicker* ideology (white supremacy) that is central to far-right parties across Europe and North America. Trump's populism works, if we follow the dominant reading of populism in political science, because it translates white identity into an imagined 'pure people,' and as outgroup hostility grows, it is anger towards the Democrats—the imagined 'elites'—that grows. Populism as a thin ideology, then, can be helpful in drawing out the discursive, ideational, and rhetorical strategies that Trump uses. It is not, however, a description of his ideology, which is unambiguously far-right and white supremacist.

2.2 Populism and Transgression

There is a problem with the ideational approach to populism. Populism provides a schema that organizes society into two camps, the people and the elite, and sees them as opposed. This is present well across the political spectrum. Bernie Sanders could certainly be considered a left-wing populist, not least for seeing society as the 99% against the 1%. That is why the ideational approach has to qualify populism as a thin ideology, because all it really posits is the antagonism between two social strata. When populism is attached to an ideology, it gives meaning to 'the people,' 'the elite,' and the 'general will.' It is a thicker ideology that makes sense of what is morally good and what is not. That is why political scientists can compare Bernie Sanders as a populist social democrat candidate on the left and Donald Trump as a populist radical right candidate. We cannot really isolate thin populism from the thicker ideology with which it is entangled when we think of populism as a set of ideas, which is more or less also how we think about ideology. If populism is abstract until its conjunction with a thicker ideology, then it is the latter that matters. Trump's populism is not, in itself, a threat to democracy. He is a threat to democracy because he represents and advances far-right ideology. The problem with the term populism, then, is that it becomes very easy to equate populism with the far right (as Brown and Mondon 2021 find) and focus on the former as a threat to democracy.

Populism tells us something about how Trump's far-right politics *work*. The sociocultural approach to populism can help us to better disentangle populism and ideology. Where the ideational approach conceives of populism as a thin ideology, the main exponents of the sociocultural approach argue that populism should be understood as a social and cultural style. This approach also espouses the idea that populism only works in conjunction with specific kinds of ideologies (to which it is essentially agnostic). Pierre Ostiguy (2017), among others, is one of the key thinkers developing this approach (see also Ostiguy, Panizza, and Moffitt 2021). He adds the cultural high and low as an orthogonal axis to the classic left-right political spectrum. This cultural axis refers to "ways of *being* and *acting* in politics" (Ostiguy 2009, p. 5 in Aiolfi 2022, p. 4). Populism, then, is the "flaunting of the low," referring to performances that express proximity to 'the people' as well as the kind of coarseness and vulgarity that characterizes Trump's transgressive style (Bucy et al. 2020; Ostiguy 2017; Aiolfi 2022, p. 5). In this sense, we can conceive of populism as a performance in politics that *violates* what is considered 'proper' and 'acceptable' in normal politics. On the populist right, the well-coiffed, cautious, and mannered comportment of elites—the epitome of 'political correctness'—is challenged by political entrepreneurs that call themselves "mavericks" or "outsiders" who "tell it like it is" without all the useless pomp and circumstance of the political establishment. The binary that Ostiguy creates also presents its own risks. By describing a duality between high and low, not unlike the false binaries drawn between 'vulgar' popular culture and 'proper' high culture by elitist cultural theorists in the 20th century (Macdonald 2006), the socio-cultural approach situates populism as something that appeals to those 'deplorables.'

What is particularly valuable about Ostiguy's argument is that it associates populism with transgression. This is an argument made by Aiolfi (2022) that is particularly notable because it identifies how the false binary between 'high' and 'low' culture represents subjective cultural dimensions. Instead, Aiolfi (2022) argues that populism is actually about transgression, or the violation of specific norms, and is a culturally neutral and observable feature of political performances. According to Aiolfi, there are three kinds of norms that populists violate: (1) norms about how "a politician ought to behave toward their peers," such as maintaining mutual respect between candidates on a debate stage; (2) rhetorical norms, such as political correctness and the appropriate manner of speaking and presenting oneself within the context of a given country; and (3) theatrical norms, or the 'tacit agreement' between candidates not to reveal the 'artificial' and staged nature of the political stage. Trump violates the latter, for example, "where Trump sarcastically praised Clinton's avoidance of a difficult question on open borders by saying 'that was a great pivot'" (Aiolfi 2022, p. 8; Blake 2016). By "breaking the fourth wall of political performances" (Aiolfi 2022, p. 8), Trump makes a joke out of his opponent and casts the political process itself as a farce.

This argument is primarily concerned with how politicians enact populism as they seek to win votes. However, this conceptualization of populism as transgression—of the violation of the 'rules of the game'—provides a compelling way for us to elucidate how Trump, the carnival fool, puts populism to work. It also helps us comprehend the different ways that the ideational and sociocultural approaches to populism can help us better understand the far right today. Trump's carnival is a celebration of the transgression of all the rules and norms of democracy. However, these transgressions and violations go well beyond Trump on the debate stage or his Twitter or Truth Social account. His transgressions encourage others to do the same. In this sense, carnival is a participatory culture of transgression that represents, at least in the case of Trump, a key aspect of how far-right politics *work*. Transgression is not, on its own, an ideology or inherently right-wing, or associated with 'bad manners' or 'low' culture. Here, transgression is done in the name of a 'pure people' against the rules of the 'elite' that renders them victims. *This* populism better explains Trump, the great 'outsider,' erstwhile reality TV star and real estate mogul, transformed into the champion of the far right violating all the liberals' foolish rules. This carnivalesque populism, of displaced abjection, misogyny, and liberation from 'political correctness,' is fundamental to understanding how

Trump's populism erodes democracy. We are not interested in defining populism as such, but rather in trying to define Trump's version of populism. His populism is chiefly concerned with transgression against the norms of democracy—defended by a set of 'elites'—on behalf of an imagined community that feels under threat and expresses outgroup hostility. As a candidate and as the president, Trump espoused a form of populism that serves as a vehicle for the far right. His carnivalesque populism, as we discuss in the next section, brings together participatory culture, anti-elitism, anti-intellectualism, and white identity to negate democratic values of equality and liberty.

2.3 Carnivalesque Populism

Carnival is quintessentially populist because of how it violates the norms and values of the elite. This elite, as with populism, is of course contingent on the society that engages in carnival. For Bakhtin, the specific characteristics of carnival culture stem from the anti-hierarchical push of popular culture against the official. Thus, it is intrinsically anti-elitist, a key feature of populism (Taggart 2002; Mudde 2004; Canovan 1999). As we mention above, while definitions of populism abound, most scholars agree that populist movements juxtapose the 'pure people' against the 'corrupt elite' (Mudde 2004; Kaltwasser and Taggart 2016), which makes the carnival framework analysis especially poignant in light of the perceived advent of the 'populist Zeitgeist.' Even though if it is intended to be short lived, carnival represents a power transfer to 'the people' from the established ruler (Bakhtin 2015). It is designed to assuage a discontented populace by creating an *illusion* of power of the masses. This makes carnival very suitable for analysis of the Trump campaign given that his persona is that of a quintessential simulacrum of a 'popular' candidate.

Given its anti-elitist nature, carnival allows for 'low culture' to come to the high world (of politics), wherein everyone is allowed to curse and swear without societal sanction. Swearing is common among carnival fools that have previously entered politics and were considered populist. It is worth mentioning that Italian comedian, actor, blogger and politician Beppe Grillo founded a Vaffanaculo-Day ["fuck off day"], abbreviated as V-Day, which despite its obscene name, served a genuine political purpose in mobilizing support for popular legal initiatives. Another 'carnival fool,' Vladimir Zhirinovksy, a late Russian far-right politician and the leader of "Liberal Democratic Party of Russia" is famous for calling his female parliamentary colleagues "bitches," reflecting a tendency for coarse and vulgar language—*ploshchadnyi* in Bakhtin's native Russian or "billingsgate" in Iswolsky's translation (Bakhtin 1968). Carnival gives license to a type of interaction unthinkable in real life, with no class or income distinction. Carnival culture can thus be seen as a counterpoint to the notion of 'civilizing' in post-medieval Europe that seemingly internalized 'self-restraint' and decreased the threshold for shame (Elias and Hammer 1979).

Carnival is fundamentally about transgression, which Bakhtin idealizes. He glorifies popular culture and the anti-authoritarian drive of the people in the carnival square. Hence, his argument that those in power never "speak the language of laughter," because laughter helps transgress taboos and fear (Bakhtin 2015):

> Seriousness in class culture is official, authoritarian, combined with violence, prohibitions, and restrictions. In such seriousness, there is always an element of fear and intimidation. In medieval seriousness, this element dominated sharply. Laughter, on the other hand, meant overcoming fear. There are no prohibitions and restrictions created by laughter. Power, violence, authority never speak the language of laughter. (p. 45)

The grotesque is also a key notion in the carnivalesque. Bakhtin uses this term quite frequently to refer to the over-the-top practices of carnival, exaggerations in costumes, acts, speech, and gestures. The grotesque emphasizes a culture of the people, not created by the elite—the inversion of the 'sanitized' world. In the "aesthetics of the monstrous," the elite's hold on the culture seems no longer visible. The grotesque offers a new perspective on the world that helps realize the relative nature of all that exists (Bakhtin 2015). However, while carnival promises joyous renewal, it may well deliver something less desirable (Danow 1995)—practices of displaced abjection, for instance (more on that below).

Transgression depends upon the existence of a norm or a prohibition. Without the rule, there is nothing to violate. Trump's frequent transgression of the norms of political culture, from showcasing his misogyny or speaking "the truth" about "radical Islam," are all targeted at violating democratic norms. This is a central aspect of Aristotle Kallis's work describing how fascist and far-right discourse *licenses* hate as a form of self-defense (Kallis 2013):

> The taboo nature of the far right's language on immigrants and immigration as a whole [...] is relativized through the imageries of threat and of the ensuing right to self-defense vis-à-vis an ostensible existential threat. Through these mutually reinforcing imageries, an array of more fundamental, previously suppressed and delegitimized prejudices appear to gain a putatively (more) legitimate lease on life and come once again to the fore [...] the prescribed transgressive behavior (discrimination, violence, expulsion, and so on) is presented as a conditional, legitimate, and targeted derogation of mainstream norms. (p. 233)

As we discuss, carnival laughter is a transgression against specific prohibitions and restrictions. Laughter in the Trump carnival is deployed to use to demonize and derogate others to re-establish the very structures and hierarchies that marginalize groups in the US. Trump is the carnival fool that puts transgression to work for the far right by violating the norms of democracy. One of the main ideas of carnival is the idea of renewal, and Trump (or, most likely, his advisor Steve Bannon) promised a rebirth of the American political system through his candidacy. It is no wonder that Trump and his surrogates consistently pushed the narrative of "outsider" (Trump) versus "insider" (Clinton) or campaigned against the "coastal elite" and "Washington DC swamp"—all of these tropes fit well within the carnivalesque disparagement of authority. Unlike the fleeting, temporal nature of 'traditional' carnival, where anti-establishment curses are quickly forgotten, the multiplatform nature of modern political communication allows the statements to be screenshot, recorded, replayed, re-sent, and re-contextualized, thus prolonging the carnival and making it a way of doing politics. But before we dive further into Trump's carnival, let us take a look at Bakhtin's.

Chapter 3: Carnival as Theory and Methodology

3.1 What Is Carnival?

Imagine a town square. Lots of people next to each other, often way too close, many are drunk or drinking. People are dressed in elaborate and colorful costumes, often with masks and extravagant headgear; sometimes the costumes are in disarray because of the festivities or even a secret tryst in a back alley. Some people are dancing and twirling, with meat and alcoholic drinks in their hands; musicians are playing folk and dance music. There are characters dressed as clowns and jesters, performing tricks and entertaining the crowd. You can watch a little carnival play performed by some travelling actors or buy a virility potion from a quack doctor. Make a fart joke or sing off tune if you like. It is ok to grab someone's buttocks or breasts if you fancy them. But don't be late for an effigy burning later, as well as more food, more alcohol, and more sex. Take it all in now, tomorrow it will be over.

The description above, with some updates, could be easily applied to a carnival in modern Europe, but Bakhtin developed the concept of carnival culture while analyzing François Rabelais's work and its connection to the popular laughing culture of the (European) Renaissance (Bakhtin 2015). At the same time, carnival also bears "the stamp of a dateless antiquity" (Frazer 2012), celebrating the body, the senses, and unofficial relations among human beings (Danow 1995). A quintessentially populist phenomenon, carnival has been an object of study for some time, but it was Bakhtin who elevated it to an epistemological category that has been applied mostly in literary studies, anthropology, history, and, more recently, political science. The vast literature on carnival's origins usually converges on the carnival being related to rituals of public expulsion of evil, common world-wide and not just in medieval Europe (Frazer 2012). In European culture, carnival's origins have been traced to ancient Greek celebrations of Dionysus that involved excess drinking and copulation (Rudwin 1919) and to Roman holidays of Saturnalia that incorporated some sort of hierarchy reversal, with slaves being allowed to don their masters' clothing and eat at the festive table (Marquardt 1963). Another antecedent, of a more religious nature, that seemed to have blended into the Rabelaisian tradition was the northern French custom of the Feast of Fools, *festum fatuorum* (Gilhus 1990), popularized for a general audience through the Disney adaptation of *The Hunchback of Notre-Dame*. The Feast of Fools involved a brief social revolution—in which power, dignity, and impunity were briefly conferred on those in a subordinate position—in elaborate theatrical performances (Harris

2011), and the celebration of marginal biblical tales and characters, for instance, donkey-related stories from the Bible.

How did Bakhtin develop the notion of carnival and the carnivalesque? He first started making notes about "the carnival of words"—his translation of "lexikalischer Karneval"—in a draft book titled "The Idea of Carnival: The Stylistic Image of Rabelais as the Carnival of Words" (Popova 2009), in which he built on German and French scholars of Rabelais and connected him with the Russophone tradition of laughing culture (Pan'kov 2010). Bakhtin was drawing a genealogical line from Menippean satire to medieval and Renaissance folklore laughing culture. Popova notes that it was an incidental interest in the issues of celebration, ritual, and the archaic origins of imagery fashionable in the 1920s-1930s that ultimately contributed to the elements of the theory of carnival (Popova 2009). Bakhtin's framework, however, rests on the 'distilled' Western European carnival practices that by the time of Gargantua and Pantagruel had already blended pagan and Christian traditions. Carnival culture emerged as an antithesis to the serious culture that was appropriate for a world dominated by religious and social doctrines. Renaissance folk, just like modern people, needed an outlet for their non-serious feelings and discourse and the Church allocated a time for folly for about three months each year (Bakhtin 2015). Carnival, in its essence, is a reversal of the 'real life': it allows one, for a short period of time, to experience the freedom individuals are usually deprived of, and to build a second identity in an alternative world. Carnival allows transgression, violation, violence, coitus, gluttony—whatever the official and real life is supposed to forbid and frown upon (Bristol 2014). In a sense, the notion of carnival is very close to the postmodern understanding of the world with its subversion and re-interpretation of existing social relations and norms (Murphy 1999). It is also close to the notion of simulacra (Grinshteyn 2000): a person within the carnival culture is defined by what they seem to be, not by what they are.

The carnival ethos was the antithesis of the 'official' and 'serious' Church-sanctioned and feudal culture; it brought out folklore and different genres of laughter that Bakhtin calls carnival. This culture is distinguished from the official buttoned-up discourse by its anti-ideology and anti-authority themes and is characterized by coarseness and vulgarity. These features are often associated with "the common people" or "plebeian society" (Bristol 2014). But for Bakhtin, the folkloric nature of carnival and its laughter vis-à-vis the authority culture was extremely valuable. In other words, carnival was for Bakhtin, a scholar in exile amid mass repressions, a benevolent manifestation of an anti-establishment drive. As Bakhtin notes, "[people] do not contemplate the carnival—they live in it, and they live in everything, because in its idea it is universally popular [i.e., for all people]" (Bakhtin 2015). During the carnival you can only live according to its laws, that is, according to the laws of carnival freedom. Later literary scholars pointed out that Bakhtin's terminology, especially that related to the notion of 'folk' (*Narodny*, people's), was a sign of "terminological mimicry," with the Soviet state's rhetoric and especially with Stalinism (Boyarskaya 2015), that often reflected Bakhtin's idealized view of the popular.

Another dangerous aspect of the 'folk' and 'popular' side of carnival is its complete disregard for authority and expertise. Remember the quack doctor from the town square? He is perceived as having the same if not more authority than a real doctor (Erickson 2021). Granted, jade vagina eggs from Hollywood actresses would always find their customers, especially in the carnival square, but during a pandemic where the vast majority of experts issue expert advice, calls for 'freedom' (again, very carnivalesque) can literally be a death sentence for people in close proximity. For instance, Qanon, with its antisemitic blood libel roots, has prided itself in questioning the world-wide consensus on COVID-19 (Erni and Striphas 2022). This makes carnival even closer to populism as it is also anti-expertise. Attacks on Anthony Fauci (the 'face' of the expertise), ignoring what experts say, anti-masking, corona conspiracies, people choosing to take horse medication instead of tested medications or other 'miracle cures' sold on Instagram, Gab, Vkontakte, TikTok or Facebook (Ball and Maxmen 2020)—these are just some of the examples of the way anti-covid activists made sense of the pandemic in a carnivalesque way.

Edelman (1988) noted that carnivalesque elements can penetrate political discourse via outsider candidates or via the candidates who at least style themselves as such. James Janack (2005) studied Russia's own Vladimir Zhrinovsky, as well as retired World Wrestling Federation grappler Jesse Ventura's effective campaign for the governorship of Minnesota, that succeeded in large part due to his "carnival fool's role of protesting against the prevailing political system" (Janack 2006).[2] While Fetissenko (2008) offered a critique of this theoretical framework, as the "spectacle of democratic elections as a whole and the ritualized courtship of campaign events in particular [are] examples of carnival" (p. 105), this book argues that the Trump campaign went far beyond just 'familiar contact' with voters and encompassed many more carnivalesque elements. Moreover, Trump's presidential campaign and presidency in a sense became an immense accumulation of spectacles (Debord 2002), and not politics.

Bakhtin's work on carnival has been applied prodigiously in the study of movements of dissent (Çelikkol 2014). Trump's campaign was one such movement

---

2 Consistent with this ethos, during his time as a WWF wrestler, Ventura would regularly sport T-shirts emblazoned with the slogan: "Win if you can, lose if you must, but always cheat."

of dissent that incorporated those whose often violent opposition to the democratic norms were transgressive. Trump raised an anti-establishment battle-cry; it came to epitomize dissent as a means of rallying voters against his opponent, who was portrayed as mainstream and experienced—part of the "Washington DC swamp."[3] At the same time, Hoy (1994) mentions that carnival's potential for political rebellion is limited—though this could be inferred from Bakhtin as well, as carnival by its nature is a temporary phenomenon, of which its participants are well aware (Bakhtin 2015). In Trump's case this temporality was particularly well taken up by his supporters, who consistently insisted that Trump's most outlandish statements and actions were just for show, and that he would be a different, "more presidential" person once in office (Zito 2016; Roller 2016).

As several scholars have noted, carnival can also be perceived as a vehicle for a post-colonial understanding of the subaltern's voice (Gardiner and Bell 1998; Mukhopadhyay 2004), "with its attention focused on the micro-politics of sanctioned and undermining cultural norms, licit and illicit language, spoken and unspoken (but performed) utterance" (Gardiner and Bell 1998, p. 113). Carnival culture's "emphasis on the transgression of cultural norms and values by subaltern groups [is] the ideal critical tool for approaching all kinds of social and material interactions" (Humphrey 2000). In many ways, carnival views transgression as necessary and righteous because it is supposed to battle against a social order that the transgressors believe are oppressing them. (Kallis 2007). Even though Donald Trump, as a white, straight, rich male could hardly be seen as subaltern, he nevertheless managed to galvanize a substantial amount of support among the American population by marketing himself as an anti-establishment figure, in other words, a subaltern voice, by using elements of the carnival culture. Perceptions of subalternity can vary among different populations (Morozov 2015), thus even white voters can perceive themselves as disenfranchised and having insufficient access to modes of representation (Chattopadhyay and Sarkar 2005). Even though carnival culture reverses conventional hierarchy, it still works to maintain the status quo because of its inherent temporality. However, while temporary rule suspension was originally intended to reinforce the existing normative order, a long-lasting carnival can have disastrous consequences for a political community, especially one whose norms are designed to protect marginalized groups. What is most important is that carnival has specific *practices* of transgression, specifically laughter, cursing words, and vulgarity. The following parts of this chapter will examine the defining features of carnival and their applicability to the study of election campaigns.

---

3 It is notable that "drain the swamp" was one of Mussolini's promises.

3.2 Carnival as Analytical Framework

White and Stallybrass (1986) wondered why carnival had taken on such an epistemological value. They concluded that as an analytic category, it catered to the generalized economy of transgression and the high/low juxtapositions of the whole social structure. However, it is the critique of the carnival framework by literature experts that makes it applicable to the study of political phenomena. The sanctioned nature of the subversion shows that the inversion of hierarchy is not total and some stratified relations remain, with minorities and women not necessarily escaping the existing power structures.

Bakhtinian carnival exacerbates the antagonistic nature and structure of carnival (Coronato 2003), even though it did not and does not bring out the full potential of anti-hierarchy, because, as Umberto Eco has argued, the disruption of rules reinforces the laws, as carnival parodies existing rules with an *authorized* transgression (Eco 1984). As Donna Stanton notes in Bareau,

> The carnival also served to contain impulses toward more radical challenge. It could be viewed as a contestatory, chaotic ritual that paradoxically helped to sustain, even to reinforce, the dominant order. (Bareau 1987, p. 129)

While the carnival framework is extremely popular in political analyses of the movements of dissent, it is remarkable that Bakhtin's theory of the carnivalesque has often been reduced to the notion of transgression. But carnival cannot be reduced to just transgression. Its other features—e. g., the multidirectional discourse, the sanctioned nature of the transgression, and especially practices of displaced abjection—make the framework much more complex. Highlighting these aspects is crucial to the understanding of carnival. This book aims to address this caveat by showing how certain more entrenched power structures remain intact within the carnivalesque reversal and, to an extent, are even amplified in regard to the issues of displaced abjection and superficial 'freedom' from political correctness. Accordingly, this book will focus on the characteristics that have made carnival an attractive framework through which to study protests (multidirectional discourse, anti-establishment, language specificity, materiality), but at the same time highlight the features that conflict with Bakhtin's original idealistic perception of carnival (displaced abjection, misogyny) but were developed by other scholars.

Bakhtinian carnival theory allows for the adoption of a holistic approach to the study of political communication during the Trump campaign that encompasses the changed circumstances of media ecology. Not only does carnival emphasize the role of multidirectional discourse, but it also underlines the multiplicity of actors involved in the cultural production of Trumpspeak, from established media personalities to anonymous 4chan users, showcasing the dangers of a populist discourse in a democratic society. Moreover, methodologically, the carnival framework fosters a multi-method approach that involves discourse and visual analysis, as well as reflection on everyday practices and their reversal that leave a mark on political institutions.

Based on the carnival framework of social reality, several important aspects need to be studied. Firstly, if carnival is an analytic framework, then the multidirectional discourse is more of a theoretical underpinning that takes us from the physical square that Bakhtin envisions to the digitally enabled carnival in which people participate through media(tion), and shows us how social media in particular serve as a carnival square for his 'foolery.' Multidirectional discourse not only establishes the setting, including platforms, modes, and agents of communication, but it also has implications for democracy, marginalized groups, and political community. Subsequent empirical chapters deal with more concrete applications of the carnival framework and highlight its main features: displaced abjection (Chapter 5), laughing culture (Chapter 6), misogyny (Chapter 7), and sex (Chapter 8). The displaced abjection and misogyny chapters demonstrate how transgression against the taboos of political correctness is central to Trump's self-presentation. The laughter chapter tells us about the practice of transgression, and the discourse around sex showcases carnival's false promise of bodily liberation. In order to apply the idea of multidirectional discourse, the empirical chapters of this book will be divided into three main parts: discourse analysis of Trump's campaign rallies, interviews, and Tweets; mainstream media coverage; and their interpretation in far-right networks.

3.2.1 Multidirectional Discourse

An important feature of carnival is its refusal to accept an official authoritative discourse that claims absolute truth. Instead, the carnival square is filled with a multitude of voices, varying genres and levels of obscenity. Elliot (1999) opines that carnivalesque language disrupts the privileged order in polite utterances by including all sorts of colloquialisms (see also Hall and White 1993), including voices that are unwelcome in polite society for a reason—in the case of Trump's campaign, this meant featuring so-called alt-right rhetoric usually limited to the fringes of discourse. Moreover, a number of Republican politicians have long lamented the fact that the United States as a country has been constrained by political correctness—Trump himself insisted "political correctness is killing this country" already in 2013 (Lopez 2016). Thus, violation of political correctness is seen as truth-telling and independence from the establishment, a necessary transgression that carnival emboldens. But carnivalesque multidirectional discourse enabled this type of rhetoric, and Trump successfully amplified it. The Trump campaign, deployed in a multiplatform media ecology, created an illusion of familiarity and a flattened hierarchy, paralleling the intimacy of the market square. However, with a kind of mediated market square, we are no longer talking about crowds but instead focusing on publics that often intersect due to the transmedia flows of information.

> Bakhtin's theories [...] cohere most in their mission to defend the integrity of the unfamiliar voice—whether it belongs to a 16th-century red-faced peasant or a sorrowing Indian widow. Bakhtin's presentation of carnival is not a prescription or a realization of utopian ideals; it is itself an artistic response, ambivalent and aimed at transforming not actual conditions but the ways of thinking of his hearers. [...] through awareness and creative manipulation of diverse modes of discourse, individuals can effect changes in their lives and beings when freedom of action is limited—a condition of life even in non-repressive societies. (Elliot 1999, 137)

Elliot's view of carnival is very close to Bakhtin's own idealistic view of the popular culture that he saw as inherently democratic and full of emancipatory potential. Indeed, much of the research on the movements of dissent in political science focuses on the anti-hierarchical carnivalesque elements that have some, if limited, potential for political change. Instead, multidirectional discourse can amplify the voices that seek to destroy the political community altogether and exclude the voices of others once and for all.

Another important characteristic of carnival is that the boundaries between performers and spectators are blurred. This is equally true of modern (political) communication, when the focus is no longer on consumers, but prosumers of content (Humphreys and Grayson 2008; Beer and Burrows 2010), which we discuss in the subsequent chapters. The participatory nature of media ecology has contributed to some foundational shifts in the way information is produced, consumed and regurgitated.[4] A typical example in this regard would be memes, available from websites wholly dedicated to providing these to users who then select an image and add text to their liking. Memes were a particularly important tool in the 2016 presidential election, to such an extent that the Trump and Clinton campaigns were often described as engaging in a World Meme War (Schreckinger 2017).

A foundational feature of carnival is its ritualistic nature that relies on certain tropes and practices that are repeated on a regular basis. Carnival participants are perfectly aware of what they are in for, because despite its perceived lawlessness, carnival period follows a very clear pattern, including a clearly delineated and an-

---

4 This issue will be addressed in more detail in Chapter 3.

ticipated end. Thus, carnival participants are grounded both discursively and practically in the existing (non)-carnivalesque features oft the event. In this regard, when Trump tried to 'channel' Nixon (the forgotten majority) and Reagan (Make America Great Again), it could be interpreted as him trying to fit within an existing political rhetoric that would have both conservative and far-right appeal. This way, Trump unleashed the carnival by violating the norms of decency and democracy. Despite him being a carnivalesque candidate, Trump still followed a certain set of rules that exist even in such a setting as carnival.

Carnival *is* multidirectional, but multidirectionality is not so much an aspect of carnival as much as it is how carnival *works*. It is the multiplicity of voices/heteroglossia that usurps authority. Trump's carnival is multidirectional, and this has as much to do with the reality of political communication and media systems because they make this multidirectionality possible. So, what matters in what we take away from Bakhtin is that carnival involves a heteroglossic structure that suspends the normal/existing stratification of communicative potential. It is then amplified and enabled by social media and the attention economy. While multidirectional discourse enables the carnival, the carnival itself has specific targets, its objects of ridicule in the laughing culture, that serve as the taboos to transgress: specifically, the abject and the feminine. We will start with the abject.

3.2.2 Displaced Abjection

An enemy in carnival culture is an enemy of carnival square freedom (Bakhtin 2015). The carnivalesque construction of enemies involves demonization, whereby "a marginalized group is degraded so as to restore specifically the core values that mainstreamers hold" (Tsukamoto 2002). Several Bakhtin critics point out that he idealized popular culture without paying sufficient attention to the fate of the real subalterns of medieval society, even though they are supposed to be elevated in the carnival's reversal of hierarchies. Historical evidence shows that carnival definitely preserved some elements of hierarchy and potentially served as an outlet to maintain the existing order, with marginalized groups being the focus of populist anger and frustration, an anger that was never actually directed at the ones in power (White and Stallybrass 1986).

In other words, in carnival culture an enemy is a focus of 'displaced abjection'—i. e., when socially 'low' groups direct their anger not against someone in authority, but towards someone (or something) of hierarchical inferiority (White and Stallybrass 1986). The idea of abjection was developed by one of Bakhtin's principal translators, Julia Kristeva (1982, p. 1):

> There looms within abjection, one of those violent, dark revolts of being, directed against a
> threat that seems to emanate from an exorbitant outside or inside, ejected beyond the
> scope of the possible, the tolerable, the thinkable. It lies there, quite close, but it cannot be
> assimilated.

Kristeva emphasized that it is the part of identity that has been rejected that creates the abject, not the actual object of abjection; it is caused by the disruption of identity, system, and order. Jews in the Middle Ages were, unfortunately, a perfect fit for this social phenomenon, especially when it came to the impossibility of assimilation mentioned by Kristeva, but abjection has been utilized in contemporary critical theory as well when some societies connote particular groups of people—mostly minority groups—as revolting figures (Tyler 2013).

Given that the abject was often symbolized by a pig, the dehumanization of Jews was intertwined with the ambiguous legacies of the pig in European culture as it served as the symbolic analogy of scapegoated groups and demonized 'others' and, in medieval tradition, primarily Jews (Komins 2001): "Like the pigs in the Venice carnival, which were chased across Piazza San Marco and stoned, in Rome Jews were forced into a race at carnival time and stoned by the onlookers." Moreover, the pig in Western culture serves to define a boundary between the civilized and the uncivilized, the refined and the unrefined. Circe's transformation into swine of rapist sailors who wandered onto her island reflects this European genealogy of the pig metaphor. As Komins (2001) notes, "the Jews who excluded themselves from the pig *carne-levare* (lifting of meat) not only became a human embodiment of the animal's festive and sinister aspects, they also were a gloomy reminder of the real abstinence of the flesh which follows the carnival season, i. e., Lent." The carnival tradition of burning or hanging an effigy (in earlier carnival traditions, even killing the mock king) is the ultimate act in achieving social inversion (Bristol 2014). Bakhtin somewhat obfuscates the dark side of the carnivalesque, with its potential for violence and death, with the idea of rebirth (Bakhtin 2015), but the lowest part of the social ladder had primarily to deal with carnivalesque cruelty.

Thus, despite Bakhtin's idealization of the popular culture, the real subaltern in the context of carnival remains subaltern. The folk that reverse the hierarchy with the elite still keep certain other social groups at the very bottom of the social ladder, who remain there through carnival practices of abuse. In other words, even in a carnival reversal, certain groups do not rise to the top of the hierarchy. Or, as Lindahl notes, carnival did not destroy the hierarchy, it just re-arranged its contents (Lindahl 1996), as carnival is inherently about creating an effigy. While Bakhtin might have frowned at us for suggesting this, the emancipatory potential of carnival is always limited for the marginalized groups because of the performative violence that is exerted on the public square. This has clear implications for the Trump campaign. In a sense, for him and many of his supporters, the campaign essentially symbolized the suspension of what they could call a "libtard episteme," where they thought themselves subjugated and were justified in being violent. While it appeared as if 'the people' took control of the government, in the end the power remained in the hands of the same Wall Street or Washington elite. Apart from directing some of his abuse at a representative of the elite—Hillary Clinton—Trump still reserved a fair amount of his rhetoric to disparage marginalized communities and specifically communities of color. At the same time, Hillary Clinton was a suitable target of abuse due to another unpalatable carnivalesque characteristic—misogyny.

3.2.3 Misogyny

As a number of researchers have pointed out, Bakhtin does not discuss the topic of gender in detail (Barta et al. 2013; Ginsburg 1993), apart from pointing out the carnivalesque praise of the fertile feminine body that usually led to misogynistic satire (Byrd 1987). At the same time, the perception of the female body was sometimes interpreted as "unruly resistance to a monologizing and specularizing discourse of phallic authority" (Nell 2001). Despite carnival's emancipatory promise for women, it was still infamous for its portrayal of "senile, pregnant hags" (Russo 1986) that were supposed to symbolize the idea of rebirth. Ultimately, it did not offer a complete inversion of the male/female hierarchy as the taboos were re-deployed in an ambivalent way and it was specifically the (grotesque) female body that became the main subject of derision and laughter (Russo 1986).

Misogynistic practices related to carnival are ubiquitous. Frazer describes "burning of the witches" rituals common to Western Europe (Frazer 2012, pp. 160 – 163) that with time were supplanted by fires *sans femmes*. Nevertheless, carnival culture retained foundational elements of anti-female tropes, as "by reducing women to misogynistic stereotypes, the buffoon acts out a contempt for women grounded in the traditional belief that they are available for sexual pleasures but never to be trusted or taken seriously" (Murphy 2006). From a psychoanalytical perspective, this kind of disparagement could be interpreted as a type of castration fear before agential women (Ducat 2005), especially given that in earlier carnivalesque rituals, women took control over their bodies and decisions.

In the context of the Trump campaign, especially once Hillary Clinton became Trump's main adversary, his misogynistic rhetoric was very much in line with European medieval popular culture. The 'mauvaise femme' (wicked woman) trope (Enders 2004, 2005) emerged from the theatrical performances of 'silly stories' (*fab-*

ula ineptissima) that featured a blood libel tale with an obligatory female Christian maid who worked for Jews and was seen as a co-conspirator in ritual murder (Rose 2015). The wicked woman was supposedly equally guilty of the ritual murder allegation, not only because she worked for Jews, but because she failed to report suspicious activity. Thus, Trump's misogyny tied in neatly with his antisemitic dog-whistling, especially when he accused Hillary Clinton of secretly colluding with 'Jewish' bankers (Posner and Neiwert 2016).

While carnival epitomizes the reversion of hierarchy, other, more foundational hierarchical relationships remain intact—such as, the domination of women by men. While women are somewhat liberated from constant male control in the context of carnival, its practices are often misogynist and employ women either as objects of sexual release or as vessels of procreation—the (monstrous) womb (Coronato 2003). Both roles remain within the gender hierarchy present outside of carnival and the only difference here is the fact that a carnival square is also a *legitimate* place for erotic frivolity (Bakhtin 1968, emphasis added). In other words, the male policing of the conjugal order is somewhat suspended, but women are still objects in the male gaze or hands.

In the case of Trump's carnival, the misogyny of carnivalesque rituals is blended with the patriarchal hold on the American media ecology and society. Studies have shown that Hillary Clinton had to contend with misogynistic double standards and outright misogyny on all mainstream media fronts (Southern and Harmer 2019; Banwart and Kearney 2018; Karpf 2017; Bachmann, Harp, and Loke 2018; Harp 2019), not to mention an organized misogynistic hate-campaign on social media and image boards (Merrin 2019). Lilly Goren and Joseph Uscinski pointed out that Senator Clinton was treated unfairly during her presidential campaign in 2008 by mostly male newscasters (Uscinski and Goren 2011) and little had changed by 2015–2016. It was especially revealing that some of the prominent journalists who covered the elections and applied the double standard to Hillary Clinton in the first place, including Matt Lauer and Charlie Rose, not to mention Bill O'Reilly or former head of Fox News Roger Ailes, turned out to have been serial sexual harassers and misogynists themselves (Poniewozik and Lyons 2017).

3.2.4 Sex and Materiality

Given that carnival is antithetical to normal, highly religious and spiritual Renaissance life, it is concerned much more with the material aspects of existence. Hence, during carnival people obsess over, and are defined by, body parts, bodily functions, sex, and material objects. Jesse Ventura's wrestling nickname—'the body'—is an all too literal example, but even the supposedly anti-Trump journalists were obsessed with his hair, skin color, the size of his hands and genitals, not to mention his weight. While Foucault discussed the "body of the sovereign" and the medieval and late medieval practices of public execution that were supposed to harm the criminal's body as much as he harmed the state (Foucault 1977), carnival equalizes the bodies of all participants and brings the shamed and forbidden practices and body parts to the fore.

> It must be said that one of the leading moments in the comedy of the medieval jester was precisely the translation of any high ceremonial and rite into the material-bodily plane; such was the behavior of jesters in tournaments, at knight ceremonies, and others. (Bakhtin 2015, p. 14)

The practices of translation that Bakhtin mentioned do not constitute a monological process. While the jester seeks to invert the traditions from their official forms, in the context of the Trump carnival, mass media were often involved with the translation of Trump's material-bodily/obscene/linguistically iniquitous statements into mainstream speak (Parks 2019) and often reduced his candidacy to his body as well. Carnival is first and foremost carnal, a part of the "bodily low" as Bakhtin would say, and Trump has often used the erotic in order to shame his opponents for instance, a male opponent is not as virile, a woman is an object for the projection of masculine desire, while his own lifestyle and image are supposed to demonstrate his own strength and potency.

The figure of the trickster is central in the material-bodily plane. While a number of scholars think that the trickster is an archetype of a clever hero such as Loki, Odysseus or Robin Hood, others point out other, less flattering features, such as lasciviousness or cruelty. In the context of carnival, the trickster is not necessarily smart or cunning (Carroll 1984). He (always a he) is a tool of the carnivalesque gaiety that only serves to symbolize the alleged subversion of the hierarchy. In the now classic work of Evans-Pritchard (1967), the Zande trickster, "Ture," was seen as clever but adulterous, a thief who did the opposite of what morals would prescribe, representing society's unconscious desires. Carroll notes the trickster's "elaborate attempts to copulate with a variety of women or to gorge himself—a reflection of our own uninhibited desires for sex and for food" (Carroll 1984, p. 113). It is the trickster/jester who sets the tone for other practices of excess, proudly displaying his transgressions of etiquette, linguistics, or law.

Another inextricable part of the material carnivalesque existence is food (Bakhtin 2015). Bakhtin notes that the material and bodily substrate of the grotesque image (food, wine, reproductive power, organs of the body) is profoundly positive. Thus, the material and bodily substance prevails, as in the end the excess is more important. Food, as well as other elements, is supposed to be present in an excessive, grotesque way: it is the food that is supposed to be gorged on, consumed without regard to the future. It is important to note that food has significant religious connotations (e. g., sacraments), but is also associated with 'guilty pleasures' and the perception of gluttony as a sin (Coveney and Whit 2000). That is why it was bound to become a significant part of carnival culture: as a sacrament, it had to be reversed into the material culture of gluttony and pleasure normally condemned outside of the carnival. The consumption of specific foods by politicians is an important part of political spectacle (Marvin 1994; Marvin and Ingle 1999). However, such ritualistic eating is not without risks. A cultural miss-step can sometimes lead to calamitous results, as UK politician (and, at the time, leader of the Labour Party) Ed Miliband, infamously photographed consuming a bacon sandwich during 2014 local elections, would attest when the image was widely circulated during the 2015 general election campaign. In American politics, the types of food and the setting of the meals are very closely observed for the signs of "being close to people" (Obama's Dijon mustard) and authenticity (Elizabeth Warren's corndog). One wrong bite, and a candidate may lose an entire state (McCarron 2019). It is worth noting that the original "Pizzagate" scandal was about a 2016 presidential candiate John Kasich eating a pizza with a fork.

3.2.5 Language: Cursing and Laughter

Stand-up comic Lenny Bruce, an American icon of freedom of speech in 1950s and 1960s, was popularized in the 21st century by the hit Amazon show "The Marvelous Mrs. Maisel." Bruce was put on trial and essentially banned from a number of US cities for the use of profanity in his routines that some researchers characterized as quintessentially carnivalesque (Damon 1997). His performances were not only distinctive in their embracing of sexual themes but also the use of swearwords, both of which were heavily policed in public spaces in the US and are still censored on TV. A documentary about his life entitled "Swear to Tell the Truth" reflects the carnivalesque belief that obscenity being the language of the populace is uniquely equipped to speak truth to power (Bakhtin 2015), while "laughter is one of the essential forms of the truth" (Bakhtin 1968, p. 66).

This combination of obscenity and laughter as conveying an impression of authenticity stems from the carnivalesque tradition. While describing Lenny Bruce as vulgar was intended to discredit him, it is essentially a compliment in a carnival. "Every speaker is a pig, every speech a vulgarity, every joke is an obscenity," cites Rudwin (1919) describing carnival in Germanic lands. Rabelais's characters quaff and gorge in medieval France, while enjoying a similar license for linguistic levity, as a vital part of the market square discourse is its liberation from the official, sanctioned, polite form. Bakhtin refers to it as "billingsgate" or "coarse and raw" language:

> Unceremonious billingsgate speech is quite frequently characterized by swearing, that is, swear words and whole swear expressions, sometimes quite long and complex. Swearing is usually grammatically and semantically isolated in the context of speech and is perceived as a complete whole, like proverbs. Therefore, curses can be spoken of as a special speech genre of the unceremonious billingsgate speech. By their genesis, curses are not homogeneous and had different functions in the conditions of primitive communication, mainly of a magical, spellbinding character [...] [In this context] they contributed to the creation of a free, carnivalesque atmosphere and a second, laughing, aspect of the world. (Bakhtin 2015, p. 12)

The genealogy of obscenity is quite long and complex, dating back to early belief systems as well as their Christian instantiation of wishing ill of somebody, often involving magic and witchcraft (Frazer 2012). Owing to their forbidden nature, it is no wonder that their use was a subject of strict social control (McDonald 2014). Moreover, in medieval culture, cursing was considered a female practice connected to misfortune. It was women who were primarily accused of and prosecuted for witchcraft. *Malleus Maleficarum*, the handbook of witch prosecution, specifically singled out its feminine nature (*maleficarum*, not *maleficorum*) and reflected the misogyny of the underlying social structure. But given that carnival suspends the everyday religious order, curses and obscenities seem to no longer have their power and are part of the inversion and subversion of the world, contributing to the grotesque.

Danow notes that the most significant weapon of the medieval grotesque is laughter (Danow 1995, p. 36), but the laughing culture of carnival is ambivalent. It is not an individual activity, but rather, it is best interpreted as a mass emotional contagion that is not reflexive and spreads quickly through crowds (De Gelder et al. 2004; De Gelder 2006). "'Official' authority is subverted most of all by laughter, a current of slippery ambivalence" (Elliot 1999, p. 130). Jesters or tricksters who are allowed to speak their mind regardless of subordination are a good example of the way carnival works. The carnival fool, a madman, or clown is supposed to serve as a short-lived regent (Danow 1995), a king for laughs (Bakhtin 2015). Proper names are replaced by nicknames, there is a high degree of familiarity: you can slap each other on the shoulder, or even on the stomach (Bakhtin 2015). This appealed to the inherent intimacy of carnival interactions: carnival participants are on a familiar footing with each other regardless of their social standing (Bristol 2014; Burke 1978; Bakhtin 2015). Moreover, the town square as the focal point of the assembled masses shrinks the spatial continuum.

When James Twitchell decried the "trashing of taste" in America in the 1990s, he compared it to carnival culture that trades in *reductio ad obscenitatem* (Twitchell 1993). This stands in stark contrast to Bakhtin's own understanding of carnival as a more truthful, more freethinking culture that is liberated from the confines of authority and the Church. It is inadvertently Bakhtinian that late-night comedy shows have become a staple of the American news landscape, where jesters like Jon Stewart or Stephen Colbert are universally considered to be more authentic than traditional pundits on mainstream TV (Hart 2013). By using carnivalesque language, engaging in the grotesque on a daily or weekly basis, late-night comedians accidentally laid the ground for the transformation of political communication as a whole into a carnivalesque space. As Bakhtin noted (2015), contemporary swearing has the same embodied and sexualized angle. If you send somebody on an erotic hike (i.e., tell a person to go fuck themselves), you are lowering the conversational plane to the grotesque level, to the body's bottom or to the places of the body where the person is born. If you send them to where they came from, it is a wish for the addressee to die, but nowadays that meaning is lost and only comes back in the carnivalesque interpretation.

Carnival, because it is multidirectional, enables a wide range of voices to engage in transgression, but it is the carnival fool, Trump, that directs this transgression at specific taboos: racism and gender equality. The next chapter, on multidirectional discourse, shows us how the transgression is executed and how Trump enables it. What matters is that by making it transgressive, Trump is making the far right *cool* and *edgy* and even *innovative*. This is the crux of his mainstreaming, how he makes politics carnivalesque and licenses anti-democratic transgression.

Chapter 4: Trump's Digital Carnival: Media and Multidirectional Discourse

In November 2015, Donald Trump retweeted a fake graphic about African-American crime statistics (Hawley 2017; Sommerlad 2019), a favored 'information' style for the far right and white supremacists online from the neo-Nazi Internet forum Stormfront to the more mainstream alt-right publications. This wasn't a one off; Trump frequently retweeted alt-right, white supremacist, and other extremist users both before and after his presidency. On January 22, 2016, Trump retweeted a user with the handle "@WhiteGenocideTM," making a joke about Jeb Bush (Kopan 2016). It is well known that 'white genocide' was a far-reaching keyword for the alt-right online that would frequently argue that multiculturalism, diversity, and immigration are in fact a conspiracy to decimate the 'white race' (see, *inter alia*, Deem 2019; Ganesh 2020). These demographic conspiracies have long been a staple of white supremacist media, from the print work studied by Abby Ferber (1998) to the web cultures that scholars such as Jessie Daniels (2009) and Les Back (2002) have analyzed. Trump also retweeted Britain First's propaganda about violence and vandalism perpetrated by Muslims, which had nothing to do with Muslims or migrants (Sommerlad 2019). On July 2, 2016, Trump's account posted a picture mocking Hillary Clinton's campaign, embellishing the image with a red Star of David and text reading, "Most Corrupt Candidate Ever!" When challenged, a Trump staffer insisted that the six-pointed star was actually meant to represent a "Sherriff's badge" star, not the Star of David despite the background featuring $100 bills re-inforcing this antisemitic trope (see Sommerlad 2019). Trump did not get much better during the presidency; in June 2020, Trump even retweeted a video of a supporter shouting "White Power" before later deleting it (BBC News 2020).

We do not present these retweets as evidence that Trump is some kind of white supremacist. These retweets represent a fundamental aspect of the Trump carnival: the role of *multidirectional discourse*. As we discussed in the introduction, multidirectional discourse is central to Bakhtin's ideas about the carnival, which he imagines as a townquare with a cacophony of voices that disrupts the polite, aristocratic order of Medieval society. Reading Rabelais, it is doubtful that Bakhtin ever conceived of the multidirectional discourse that the contemporary American media sphere affords today. These retweets prefigure the point we wish to make in this chapter: that the carnival square is not necessarily a *physical* space in which the carnival takes place. Thanks to digital media systems, and social media in particular, we see that the carnival square is not fixed in space or time, but rather is dispersed across both dimensions. If we are to discuss a Trump carnival, then we must conceive of it as a *digital carnival,* one that brings a multiplicity of voices to the fore.

As the carnival fool, the trickster that brings the carnival together, Donald Trump's retweeting of white supremacists reveals to us how carnivalesque politics work in the light of Trump's transgression of fundamental political rules. Not being openly supportive of white supremacists has been one of these rules at least since 1965—this strategy is not undertaken simply to "own the libs" or to post a "joke". Rather, it is a strategy that has normalized a far-right and white supremacist ideology and it depends on resonance and repetition from thousands of accounts on social media platforms and alternative media sources. As is the case with the African-American crime 'statistics,' most of the information in these tweets is a fabrication, a half-truth, or simply emotive clickbait. Trump's retweets such as these systematically integrate far-right rhetoric in the mainstream (see Miller-Idriss 2018, 2020). This tweet, and Trump's subsequent refusal to delete it or admit that it was false, legitimized alt-right voices as part of the multidirectional discourse of his campaign and consequently, the American political landscape. The "shameless normalizing" of the far-right discourse (Wodak 2019) was not the only new feature of the Trump campaign when compared to his rivals and predecessors. Ganesh (2020) developed a theory of how, specifically on Twitter, decentralized alt-right publics and politicians, including Donald Trump, attempt to 'document' anti-whiteness, legitimize white supremacist voices, and reinforce their audiences' perception of the righteousness of their indignation. Other scholars have focused on how Trump performs classic agenda-setting maneuvers through his use of social media. Responding to the veracity of these claims, such as showing that the 'statistics' Trump retweeted were completely false, plays into his hands by making his transgressions a spectacle for all, only reinforcing the perception that the fact-checkers are biased, controlled by the leftists like the rest of the 'mainstream media.'

Our perspective expands on Bakhtin's ideas about the structure of carnival, but provides a pathway to bring white supremacist ideology into dialogue with the complex sociotechnical systems that characterize the contemporary media arrangement (Bennett and Livingston 2018). What is crucial to remember is that Trump, perhaps more than any other American presidential candidate, harnessed a dispersed, active, and extreme set of voices with whom his transgressions not only *resonated* but whom he also encouraged, legitimized, and licensed—across a wide range of platforms—to engage in these transgressions in turn. It is in this complex, transmedia system that Trump's carnival operates. This provided significant advantages that enabled the carnival not to be a gathering in a square, but one that stretched across space with media and digital technology. Furthermore, instead of the ephemerality of carnival, these technologies sustained the Trump carnival over time. Indeed, it was a changing media system and new technologies —particularly social media—that enabled Trump's carnivalesque politics.

But it is important to remember that we take a transmedia perspective on the Trump carnival, which means that while social media and far-right platforms played a crucial role in creating a carnival square stretched across space and time, the TV-broadcasters and the mainstream press were also caught up in the carnival. Through this complex media system, Trump was able to broadcast his transgressions and large audiences were able to partake in their own form on social media while broadcasters and the press continued to amplify his transgressive style and far-right ideology. As we discuss in this chapter, this served to normalize Trump's far-right ideology as well as legitimize his broader narratives of white victimhood. The digital carnival would not have been possible without the extensive changes that took place in the American media system primarily due to the role of the Internet, social media, and alternative media. This chapter sets the stage for the Trump carnival by showing how carnivalesque multidirectional discourse defined political communication, emphasizing the role of social media and its implications for democracy as well as exposing important actors in the media system.

In this chapter, we situate the Trump carnival in the context of broader changes in the US media system, particularly the rise of far-right media outlets and the changing role of social media platforms. This topic itself would merit a book longer than this, so we are only able to provide an outline of some key features, particularly as they relate to the Trump carnival. First, we start by discussing the notion of marketplace in the carnival, its condition of heteroglossia, and the role of multidirectional discourse in a transmedia perspective. Second, we discuss the Trump carnival in the contemporary media system, outlining broad changes in the US media network and how they enabled an environment of transgression by incorporating a multiplicity of voices. We then discuss the idea of anonymity and the carnival mask in contemporary form as processes that normalize far-right discourse. Picking this up in the context of social media, we use trolling to illustrate how we can understand how the Trump carnival is a complex, transmedia phenomenon that enables the transgression of fundamental norms.

4.1 The Trump Carnival in the Market Square

Scholars have been discussing the challenges that traditional mass media have faced in recent years for some time (Esser and Pfetsch 2004; Bennett 2015a; Klimmt, Vorderer, and Ritterfeld 2007; Syvertsen 2003; Van Dijck and Poell 2015; Dahlgren 2003; Zhao 1997). Media's gatekeeping role and the role of the market have been especially emphasized as issues that have contributed to the immense changes to the media ecologies around the world. In the context of this book, it is important to emphasize that traditional mass media no longer have a monologic or even dialogic discursive relationship with the audience. Instead, (political) communication is primarily characterized by multidirectional discourse (Lee 2014; Wolfe, Jones, and Baumgartner 2013).

As Yates (2019) notes, the 2016 campaign was a year of "democrazy" and was more emblematic of the politics of spectacle, and not a democratic process. She further notes that the media were fixated on the coverage of extreme, personalized candidates who created spectacles and employed demagoguery. The latter was deemed particularly dangerous even by the Founding Fathers (Ceaser 2007), while a number of scholars warned against it during the 20th century, even before the advent of social media (Luthin 1951). Richard Hofstadter's quote from 1963 is particularly prescient:

> The growth of the mass media of communication and their use in politics have brought politics closer to people than ever before and have made politics a form of entertainment in which spectators feel themselves involved. (Hofstadter 1963)

In a spectacle, social media have been instrumental in skewing information streams to the benefit of demagogues and anti-democratic, alt-right voices. Fears of a "media-driven republic, in which mass media will usurp the functions of political institutions in the liberal state" (Mazzoleni and Schulz 1999) have been around for a while, and most media scholars contend that the US has reached the fourth stage of mediatization—"when political and other social actors not only adapt to the media logic and the predominant news values, but also internalize these and, more or less consciously, allow the media logic and the standards of newsworthiness to become a built-in part of the governing processes" (Strömbäck 2008, pp. 239–240). Social media are crucial in the mediatization process and as such play a pivotal role in the functioning of the democratic process. However, as journalists have found with regard to YouTube (Bergen 2019) and revelations following the documents released by whistleblower Frances Haugen (eg. Zadrozny 2021), social media platforms were aware of polarization, radicalization, and the far right on their platforms, but developed incomplete solutions or brushed these problems aside, reflecting the faults of the US media ecology in general.

In the so-called post-truth world (Parmar 2012; Stewart et al. 2016; Mocanu et al. 2015), multidirectional discourse predominates, providing a platform for Trump's carnivalesque transgression. As Elliot noted:

The function of 'official culture' reappears in the image of the 'authoritative discourse' or 'monologic discourse': a one-sided world that claims absolute truth. 'Dialogic discourse' like the image of carnival activity responds and moves [...] 'Multidirectional discourse,' meanwhile, resembles the ambivalent and subversive language of the marketplace, simultaneously debasing and renewing, revealing and hiding, selling and entertaining. (Elliot 1999, p. 133)

A carnivalesque understanding of multidirectional discourse is especially helpful for the re-conceptualization of modern media ecology in several ways. First, the notion of the marketplace is key here. The carnival framework is not only a reference to the level of interaction—the 'lowering' of the discourse, according to Bakhtin—but was especially emblematic of the Trump campaign. The notion of "coarse and raw" language (Bakhtin 2015, Janack 2006; Holloway and Kneale 2002)—curses, oaths, popular blazons, profanity—defines the carnival square (Bakhtin 2015). Stripping daily interaction from political correctness can be seen as an act against ideology and hierarchy, exactly as one would expect in a carnival environment. One should not, however, forget that the carnivalesque erasure of political correctness is not an emancipatory act, even though it is seen as such by the white cis majority. Rather, it is an act that reinforces hierarchy and the abjection that minorities face within and outside of carnival, the subject of the following chapter. While a certain level of political correctness has existed in the English language, at least since the English Reformation (Hughes 2011), it has been primarily aimed at reducing linguistic violence towards discriminated/minority groups (Cay 1998; Andrews 1996). With the billingsgate language of carnival, there is no room for the sensitivities of marginalized groups, while the ambivalence of laughter (Bakhtin 2015) and the polysemy of metaphors prevalent in carnival offer convenient excuses for dogwhistling (Moshin 2018): it was only a joke, why are you offended?

Second, carnival's marketplace foreshadows the growing commercialization tendencies in society and media consumption in particular. As Pickard (2019, 2016) notes, market forces coupled with accelerated advances in technology in the United States have decimated newsrooms and imperiled a democratic society that depends on professional journalism to inform the public. The commercialization of mass media, especially news media and the pursuit of viewership that translates into more advertising contracts and higher revenue, has had an especially profound effect on the media system. With publicity materials often substituting for content through native advertising practices, it is not always entirely clear whether a person is consuming 'legitimate' content or a marketing strategy. To Bakhtin, advertising is an important part of the multidirectional discourse, as

it is not always possible to distinguish the tones and images of trade advertising from the advertising tones and images of the farce barker, a seller of medical herbs and an actor, a charlatan, a compiler of horoscopes at a fair. (Bakhtin 2015, p. 86)

One need just remember that one of Trump's major announcements concerning his *birther*[5] convictions transmuted into a presentation of his new Trump International Hotel Washington DC, which was dutifully reported on by the mass media for hours (Nelson 2016). The Trump persona, combining elements of both the businessman and the politician, caters to the carnivalesque understanding of ambivalence , while it is the ambiguity that makes it hard to distinguish between the provision of information and the peddling of goods.

Third, simultaneous "selling and entertaining" was especially visible when one accounts for the motivation behind major American news networks in the US giving Trump so much airtime. As the former CBS CEO, Les Moonves admitted in early 2016, "the money is rolling in and this is fun [...] bring it on, Donald. Keep going" (Greene 2018). Trump's campaign was entertaining, and entertainment sells. The high ratings of late-night shows, already a staple of American TV, and the convergence of celebrity and political journalism (Boydstun and Lawrence 2019) demonstrated that Trump navigated a multitude of channels that guaranteed him optimal coverage. Trump's campaign was not an example of dialogical discourse. His tweets, rallies, interviews, and political ads were amplified, refracted, and, most importantly, covered by all major TV networks, 'quality' and 'yellow' newspapers, and on social media, which together constituted a quintessential example of multidirectional multiplatform discourse. The transmedia nature of information is a useful lens through which to study the issue of multidirectional discourse. Media narratives follow a very complex transmedia route with constant cross-pollination (Gürel and Tığlı 2014; Jenkins 2010; Gambarato 2012). Verbal discourse from major television networks and high-circulation newspapers is often transformed by the audience on social networks, and sometimes visualized through memes, thus making social network users 'prosumers,' and not just passive consumers of content. Traditional media amplify narratives that are circulating on social media. Simultaneously, blogs reflect and refract TV narratives, creating a mutually reinforcing multiplatform discourse.

Another important issue relates to the documented algorithmic bias on social networks that favors racist and far-right content (Noble 2018) and may lead to self-radicalization. Social networks have been known to balance the popularity of certain accounts and groups of users despite their violation of community guidelines, and they have generally deployed piecemeal strategies and at times a relatively light touch on the far right (see Ganesh 2021, Diaz and Hecht Felella 2022, Siapera

---

5 Birtherism is a racist campaign spreading a conspiracy theory suggesting that Obama was not born in the United States and therefore was ineligible to be president according to the Constitution, which requires the president to be a natural-born citizen.

and Viejo-Otero 2021). In other words, social networks are materially interested in locking the users on their platform by monetizing on racist and abusive content (Leidig 2023).

4.2 The Trump Carnival and the Media System

Political communication is its own scholarly field that is in itself quite wide, studying how politicians represent themselves to the electorate, forms of political advertising, and how lobby groups and political parties spread their messages and ideologies. Political communication can be defined as "the construction, sending, receiving, and processing of messages that potentially have a significant direct or indirect impact on politics" (Graber and Smith 2005, p. 479). For much of the 20th and 21st centuries, the media system was primarily organized around the press and broadcast, and even into the 2016 election, most Americans still received their news and information about politics from television and news websites (Gottfried et al. 2016). This began to change in the late 20th century, with the rise of partisan cable news, particularly in the US. The web dramatically changed this picture in the early 2000s, and by the 2010s, Barack Obama's and Narendra Modi's campaigns were among others across the world that were lauded for their deft use of social media campaigning. In the early 2000s, promissory narratives about social media corporations were ubiquitous, making dramatic claims about their potential for innovation in democracy and freedom of expression. The reality is that social media—particularly through advertising—were effective propaganda machines, for two reasons: first, their 'democratic' nature enabled an immense array of alternative information, news, and entertainment sources; second, their lax regulation for electoral campaigning, their advertising policies, and their rather naïve free speech absolutism offered a new frontier for political communication without the normal oversight that protects electoral processes. This enabled lobby groups, Democrat and Republican alike, to run thousands of advertisements without disclosing that they were paid for by campaigns or PACs (see Kim et al. 2018). But social media also enabled a kind of participatory culture in politics, transforming parties into platforms, and extracting likes, shares, and retweets as tiny acts of political labor that would allow audiences to connect with campaigns (Gerbaudo 2019; Falasca, Dymek, and Grandien 2019). And perhaps most importantly, they made it possible for alternative media—run by far-right partisans like Breitbart—to position themselves as serious competitors to established journalistic outlets.

This media system provided the perfect opportunity for populist transgression, which Trump's campaign and its adjacent alternative media system were quite successful in exploiting. Optimists were convinced of the emancipatory power of the Internet and anticipated "Twitter Revolutions" around the world and expected that the coming age of 'big data' would provide computational solutions to myriad problems (e. g., Anderson 2008), not least how to win an election (Zittrain 2014). On the face of it, platforms like YouTube that made it possible for any creator to reach a large audience promised to challenge the power of traditional gatekeepers and editors in the news industry. On the other hand (and in hindsight, of course), it is clear that by giving everyone a voice, these platforms began to erode the value of scientific expertise. Social media, then, drastically changed the possibilities for what Bakhtin refers to as multidirectional discourse or *heteroglossia*. The democratization of these platforms—while they certainly opened up space for more voices—enabled the rise of the far right as well as transnational solidarities between its partisans.

As Jessie Daniels argues, white supremacists and far-right partisans in the US have long exploited technical innovations, using new digital technologies over the course of the last four decades (Daniels 2018). In one of the most comprehensive studies of the Anglophone far right on YouTube, Rebecca Lewis demonstrates that an alternative information network, composed of microcelebrities in subcultural niches, talk show hosts, and influencers, became highly partisan sources of information to audiences on YouTube (2018). In their comprehensive work on the US media system and polarization, Benkler, Faris, and Roberts (2018) make a convincing argument that right-wing alternative media played an important role in Trump's success against other Republican competitors, catapulting the Trump wing to the forefront of the party. Central to this process is what Benkler and colleagues refer to as a "propaganda feedback loop" in which media outlets compete on the basis of identity confirmation, (rather than by presenting the truth), often conflating news and opinion. The public seeks out news that confirms their identity biases, and the media deliver favorable coverage to those politicians that conform to the identity biases of the public and the very same media outlets. The model Benkler et al develop is not designed to understand a particular side of the political spectrum, instead they convincingly argue that this feedback loop is strongest on the right in the US. This is facilitated along in an attention economy in which traditional media outlets such as broadcasters and newspapers are in competition with upstarts, such as digital media outlets including Breitbart or the Daily Caller, and a cohort of reactionary influencers that Lewis and others have studied. They argue that this propaganda feedback loop is a

> steady flow of bias-confirming stories that create a shared narrative of the state of the world; a steady flow of audiences, viewers, or clicks for the outlets; and a steady flow of voters highly

resilient to arguments made by outsiders on outlets that are outside the network. (Benkler, Faris, and Roberts 2018, p. 80)

While Benkler, Faris, and Roberts (2018) are careful to stress that Fox News plays a central role in this feedback loop, it is also clear that social media platforms have significantly reshaped the attention economy and drastically increased the incentives for identity-confirming news and the publics that seek it.

At the same time as established and new right-wing media outlets were building and expanding an identity-confirming media system, social media platforms also offered a variety of opportunities for multidirectional discourse. As many scholars have noted, the 'democratic' nature of social media platforms is only a myth as social media platforms are anything but democratic in their design (see Van Dijck, Poell, and de Waal (2018), amongst others). It significantly reduced barriers to entry for a wide range of commentators and pundits and made it possible for a broad assortment of far-right users to gain traction and audiences online (e.g., Lewis 2020; Ganesh 2018). As research into the "alt-right" has revealed in the past years, social media platforms provided an opportunity for extreme voices to gain large followings (see Ganesh 2020), which narrowed as platforms took action against them in the late 2010s (see Rogers 2020). Algorithms at these platforms played an important role in expanding the reach of these voices. For example, in an experiment Whittaker et al. (2021) found that YouTube amplified extreme content that involves stark dehumanization and calls for violence to users that engaged with more 'moderate' forms of far right content. Others who have studied such content linking for far right content on YouTube have come to similar results, with Schmitt et al. (2018) finding that the algorithms on YouTube even frustrate counter-messaging strategies, while O'Callaghan et al. (2015) observed that YouTube recommendations on extreme right content were likely to send users into a 'rabbit hole'. This was also the case on Facebook, where researchers found that "64 percent of people who joined an extremist group on Facebook only did so because the company's algorithm recommended it to them" (Statt 2020). Thus, social media platforms played a dual role: they flattened authority and enabled a whole host of extremists to establish a presence as trusted commentators and 'microcelebrities' at the same time that their algorithmic systems often supported the growth of the audiences of these extreme narratives. Thus, the 'democratic' nature, then, of social media is better understood as the enabling of a multidirectional discourse that greatly expanded opportunities for far right partisans to participate in political discourse in the country.

In opening out the possibility to reach an audience, and in a propaganda feedback loop (as Benkler, Faris, and Roberts 2018 put it), Trump's digital carnival enabled the enactment and performance of a specific kind of populism. This populism is less a referent to a 'people', but rather a repudiation of expertise and authority in favor of popular perception and belief. This enables transgressions against authority and a rejection of the claims of experts, associating the state, scientists, and civil servants as all part of an evil 'elite.' Multidirectional discourse, often pushed along by Trump, as well as other right-wing politicians, lobbyists civil society groups, influencers and microcelebrities, managed to make the use of hyperpartisan media itself a transgressive act. Beginning in the late 2010s, and especially during the coronavirus pandemic, social media platforms were pressured into action against the growth of these hyperpartisan media outlets, and they increasingly began to take down the accounts of the far-right and conspiracy theorists and those promoting COVID-19 misinformation (see De Kuelenaar, Magalhães, and Ganesh 2023). This action also became to be seen as part of the 'elite' clampdown on the voice of the people. Indeed, as research has shown, the act of ejecting these accounts from the platforms drove an economy of alternative tech platforms catering to far-right users (Donovan, Lewis, and Friedberg 2019; Rogers 2020). Just like jihadists (Pearson 2018), far-right users that were deplatformed considered their banishment from Facebook, YouTube, Instagram, and Twitter as a medal of valor, authenticating them as the *real* truth-tellers who stand up to the 'woke' elites, who certified their practices as transgression.

In many ways, Trump's populist appeal and the highlighting of fringe far-right groups and their discourse fulfilled the promise of a multidirectionality. As a gatekeeper of what could potentially make it to the national discourse, Trump became an amplifier of far-right rhetoric, even without the coded racist language that had been present in the GOP vernacular beforehand (Brown 2016). His no-longer-veiled racism was essentially an articulation of the existential anxiety experienced by the white majority over 'demographic shifts' and fears of 'replacement' that have been circulating within and outside of the American establishment for over a century. Turn-of-the-century white supremacist ideologues such as Madison Grant or Lothrop Stoddard, fearful of the disenfranchisement of the white population, warned against the "rising tide of color." Their talking points found their way again into mainstream media as Trump opened the floodgates for the tide of racist rhetoric, allowing the heteroglot perspectives of the far right to permeate political discourse, thwarting the main purpose of media in a democracy—to inform the people.

4.3 Multidirectional Discourse and Carnival Masks

Any language, in Bakhtin's view, stratifies into many voices: social dialects, characteristic groups, professional jargon, generic language, language of generations and age groups, tendentious language, language of the authorities and of various circles and passing fashions (Ball, Freedman, and Pea 2004). Heteroglossia [raznorechie] is thus a condition of language as it is deployed in varying ways to evaluate, conceptualize, and experience the world (Blackledge and Creese 2014). Despite Bakhtin's somewhat idealistic portrayal of the popular culture of Renaissance carnival, not all voices are heard in (political) communication (Spivak 1999). The true marginalized voices, the ones that become the focus of carnival's displaced abjection, remain silent and their experience of the world is excised from the general merriment of the town square. From a communications standpoint and in the case of Trumpian carnival this erasure does not take place as the multidirectional discourse of social media has ensured the presence of some marginalized voices. At the same time, the paticularities of the presidential American voting system —majority white states voting first in primaries, the existence of an electoral college, and numerous cases of voter suppression and gerrymandering—are evidence that the disenfranchisement of the American electorate is not directed at the white majority at all (Scher 2015). Moreover, if one looks at the 2016 election results by group, it becomes clear that the favorite candidate of the minority groups (e.g., Black, Latina), the subaltern voices, did not become president.

A principle promise of carnival is its seeming reversal of social hierarchy, supposedly rendering it democratic. Bakhtin himself discussed the democratic promise of carnival based on its folk roots. Other researchers note that Bakhtin's somewhat idealistic understanding of popular culture as the privileged bearer of democratic and progressive values leads to a quintessentially populist vision of Renaissance carnival culture being a harbinger of an as yet politically unrealized democracy (Shevtsova 1992; Hirschkop 1986). Moreover, Bakhtin's critics note that he romanticized popular culture and language and neglected the fact that true subalterns were never allowed to participate in a "march of the deposed gods"(2015, p. 148).

In carnival, the subjects of speech are not people, but anonyms hidden behind the masks of the discourse that constitutes them, as Julia Kristeva aptly noted (Kristeva 2000). This observation is extremely relevant for social networks, where even real people use their own accounts to cultivate a persona, sometimes whitewashing or outright lying in their posts, not to mention altering their looks by means of filters or Photoshop. Apart from a genuine person behind an account, there are a host of other possibilities, including teams of public relations specialists, automated accounts (bots), trolls assuming an online identity, paid commentators (so-called 50-cent commentary trolls), or even a suspicious spouse browsing under their partner's name. One way or another, accounts on social media can be seen as masks in the carnival with their polysyllabic and polysemantic symbolism.

As Kristeva notes, carnivalesque discourse breaks the laws of language censored by grammar and semantics (Kristeva 2000). However, this transgression is still somewhat 'controlled,' as even in the case of Trump breaking language taboos, 'transgressors' are still partially censored by mainstream media, while journalists often engage in the "translation" of Trump's linguistic mistakes and malformed sentences into digestible, conventional English, as Parks astutely observed (Parks 2019).

> The mask is associated with the joy of change and reincarnation, with cheerful relativity, with the joyful denial of identity and unambiguity, with the disavowal of stupid conformity to oneself; the mask is associated with transitions, metamorphoses, violations of natural boundaries, ridicule, and a nickname (instead of a name); the game's beginning of life is embodied in the mask, it is based on a very special relationship between reality and image, characteristic of the most ancient ritual-spectacular forms. (Bakhtin 2015, p. 26)

The mask can embolden wearers with the anonymity it provides as well as enable the expression of true feelings and the manifestation of repressed desires. No wonder that it is the mask of anonymity 'worn' by some Internet commentators that allows for vicious attacks, though of course many do not require the mask of anonymity to express hatred. Putting on a red baseball cap in a sense has become a carnivalesque act of donning a carnival costume and a mask. The red cap became an avatar for an entire ideology to such an extent that even academics published books featuring it, marking the belonging and the meaning to such an extent that there are scores of red baseball hats with completely antithetical messages on them, auch as "Made ya look: Black Lives Matter" or "Lock Him Up."

Among the masked participants of the carnival, the trickster stands out, a mythical figure whose attraction and fascination lies in an ability to embody two opposing principles within a single person (Evans-Pritchard 1967)—a selfish buffoon (Carroll 1984), who seeks the immediate gratification of physical desires, be they sexual intercourse, feasting, or excretion, but also a transformer of social relations (Martin and Jensen 2017). Being an oxymoron is a feature of the trickster figure. Thus, the usual attempt by TV pundits or late-night comedians to criticize Trump's hypocrisy have failed, because as an archetypal trickster figure he is immune to this type of criticism. As empirical chapters will show, these oxymoronic features are common in Trump's discourse. He rarely deviated from the materiality in his speech that his voters mistook for authenticity. As Bakhtin notes,

> the tricksters and fools were their constant participants and parody duplicated various moments of serious ceremonies (glorification of winners in tournaments, ceremony of transfer of feudal rights, initiations into knights, etc.). (Bakhtin 2015, p. 3)

This 'ceremonial' presence of fools that accompany serious rituals may explain why Trump's candidacy was initially welcomed by virtually all late-night comics, who saw his campaign as a source of entertainment. As a ceremonial fool, Trump was not taken seriously by his fellow primary contenders, which guaranteed him light-hearted coverage without a serious focus on his policies. There is a literature on Trump being the ultimate trickster who managed to con the American people (Martin and Krause-Jensen 2017), but whether as a genuine contender or as an unceremonious fool, Trump was a constant feature of the political communication in the 2016 election campaign. Bakhtin noted that in a trickster figure, "all the attributes of the king are turned upside down, rearranged from top to bottom; the trickster is the king of the 'inside out world'" (Bakhtin 2015, p. 140), but the inside-out world suddenly became the real world.

Given the level of mediatization (Strömbäck 2008) of American society, it is important to pay attention to the way traditional mass media responded to Trump's agenda-setting campaign efforts. As carnival is a laughing culture, it is important to include the analysis of late-night comedy as one of the voices of the multidirectional discourse. A number of researchers have emphasized the significant role that late-night shows play in American political communication (Young 2019; Hart 2013; Postman 2006; Moy, Xenos, and Hess 2005). In the spirit of carnival and the general disaffection and polarization of the American electorate, these shows were instrumental in priming and popularizing the Trump campaign. At the same time, traditional media, such as quality newspapers and regular TV news, served as fodder for the Trump campaign, which accused the 'lamestream' media and "the failing *New York Times*" of peddling misinformation.

What Trump succeeded in doing was to expand the discursive space to include normally censored voices and topics, which partly confirms Bennett's indexing hypothesis that the range of views that are covered as "acceptable or normal" by media outlets depends on the range of views expressed in Congress (Bennett 2015b). However, public spaces are becoming more and more disrupted (Bennett and Pfetsch 2018), especially through the practices of political *astroturfing* (Howard, Woolley, and Calo 2018), when lobby groups masquerade as grassroots initiatives. Through this, it is easier to manipulate the range of topics covered by the media. By framing some of his rhetoric as a backlash against so-called 'coastal elites'—a typical populist frame that juxtaposes 'pure people' against 'corrupt politicians'—the Trump campaign embodied what Ruth Wodak calls the "shameless normalizing" of the far right discourse (Wodak 2019), making far-right positions truly mainstream.[6] Trump was not alone in this endeavor. Even post-presidency,

---

6 It should be noted that white supremacy and some derivatives of far-right rhetoric have been

he managed to mainstream many extreme positions that have become part of the US Congress. Jewish space lasers, stolen elections, great replacement theories, and other conspiracy myths have now been fully entrenched on Capitol Hill.

4.4 Carnival, Social Media, and Trolling

Early theories of political communication often discarded the role of the public, who were frequently seen as passive consumers of politicians' speeches, mass media, or opinion leaders (Katz 1987). The advent of television did not change the asymmetry between politicians and their audiences that relied primarily on an allegiant model of citizenship and conventional public participation (Milbrath and Goel 1977; Campbell et al. 1960). However, with the emergence of social media platforms, changing views on political participation that gradually included active and deliberate behavior (Fox 2013) and diverging modes of political communication evolved. Social media created different ways of producing content, distributing information, and consuming media (Klinger and Svensson 2015), influencing gatekeeping and the commercialization of information.

When Shanti Elliot described carnival as a "cosmic openness" where "nothing is fixed but everything is in a state of becoming" (Elliot 1999, p. 130), she probably did not have social media in mind as they were only just beginning to sprout all over the world at the time of her writing. Yet, this portrayal is quite pertinent for the description of a digitized media system. Social networks embody this multidirectional discourse. This fast-paced and transient environment not only offers instant gratification, a very powerful psychological driver (Shao 2009; Wu et al. 2013), but also confirms the temporality of carnival. Fake news, memes, product placement, gifs, cat videos, and quality journalism co-exist on a seemingly equal footing where it is almost impossible to sort the wheat from the chaff.

Testimonies presented to the US Congress have shown that microtargeting, inflated video content viewership numbers (Machkovech 2016), and a lack of regulation of political advertising on social networks has left much room for manipulation, including by foreign powers (United States Office of the Director of National Intelligence 2017). This is extremely relevant in regard to the multidirectional nature of the carnivalesque discourse. With political advertising produced by actors outside of the American political system who masquerade as American citizens, it

observed in the US Congress for some time, with a blatant example being Republican Representative from Iowa Steve King who repeatedly endorsed white supremacy. The Republican Steering Committee only removed him from all House committee assignments in 2019, though of course Steve King is not the only member of the GOP that openly supports such extreme views.

is also clear that political communication in the US is by no means a dialogical process. It is also apparent how a mere semblance of authority, and not authenticity, is sufficient in a carnival setting (Yates 2019). In Trump's case, he succeeded in consistently attracting disaffected voters with his "impression of bare-knuckle authenticity" as a "blue-collar billionaire" (Wells et al. 2016).

Another major change ushered in by the emergence of social media relates to the illusion of closeness to the political process (Kruikemeier et al. 2013), which is fundamentally important to the carnival framework. After all, carnival is the time when "Ivan Ivanovich [formal] turns into Vanya [less formal] or Van'ka [informal]" (Bakhtin 2015, p. 11) and the market square supposedly flattens hierarchy, bringing everybody together. The ability to tweet at somebody, send them a direct message, and comment on their posts creates an ultimate populist fantasy of 'people's candidates,' even though most campaigns have teams of social media experts that come up with situationally appropriate 'burns' and 'zingers.' Donald Trump's Twitter account, with its characteristic patterns of random capitalization, semantic, lexical, and punctuation blunders and misspellings, provided a level of anti-elitism with which no other candidate—and especially Hillary Clinton—could compete (allthough her "delete your account" Tweet was a solid burn in June 2016).

Another element of 'carnival square' that suddenly became part of the main carnival square of Trump's political communication included discussion groups on Reddit as well as 'imageboards' such as 4chan and 8chan. These platforms seek to preserve the anonymity of their users, taking pride in upholding the once almost universal anonymity of the Internet during its earliest days. For instance, 4chan hosts numerous public boards dedicated to a wide variety of topics, including anime, gaming, music, fitness, politics, sports, and pornography. According to 4chan's 'Press' page, 4chan serves over 22 million users a month and as of October 2023, has approximately 4.6 billion posts in total, reported on its homepage. Registration is not possible and everybody is forced to post anonymously, with threads receiving recent replies being 'bumped' to the top of their respective board. The platform has been a significant hub for Internet subculture and activism, both from the left and from the right, but it gained notoriety specifically as a hot-bed for the so-called alt-right movement (Nagle 2017).

The anti-authority spirit pervaded the alt-right movement, amplifying Trump's bid for presidency. Their new brand of conservatism essentially rejected its more mainstream iteration in its open acceptance of white supremacy somewhat uniting neo-Nazi, populist, anti-feminist, homophobic, anti-immigration, anti-Islam, anti-semitic, and incel[7] streams. While extremely amorphous and diverse, the alt-

---

7 So-called "incel" culture refers to "involuntary celibate," an online culture whose members de-

right converged on their shared opposition to obeisance to political correctness (PC) and the supposed damage it does to the white cis majority. Unlike some of the anti-PC spaces on 4chan or Reddit, where those identifying as trolls seeking to provoke other users into an emotional reaction by their challenging of social norms, the core of the alt-right and the person who coined the term—Richard Spencer—are dead serious in their white supremacist rhetoric that has already led to mass shootings, murders, riots, and vandalism (Nagle 2017; Winter 2019). Their support for Trump has been exemplified by the endorsement of David Duke, former Grand Wizard of the Ku Klux Klan (Domonoske 2016).

'Genuine' trolling is a carnivalesque phenomenon, with the trolls' quest to 'affect authority' creating a spirit of disruption, playfulness, humor, and profanity in the 'low' discursive part of life. As Merrin notes, "trolling, therefore, is a baiting, a sport, a playing, that more than anything aims at those who get above themselves, or set themselves above others—at those asserting, or in, authority" (Merrin 2019, p. 202). The fundamental idea of carnival is the reversal of hierarchy while poking fun at those who are in authority. Trolling could be considered a hallmark of Trump's campaign, with trolls consolidating a significant part of the electorate that might not have anything to do with Internet subcultures through the so-called "Great Meme War"—that is, the flooding of the Internet with pro-Trump and anti-Clinton memes. As Schreckinger notes,

> There is no real evidence that memes won the election, but there is little question they changed its tone, especially in the fast-moving and influential currents of social media. The meme battalions created a mass of pro-Trump iconography as powerful as the Obama "Hope" poster and far more adaptable; they relentlessly drew attention to the tawdriest and most sensational accusations against Clinton, forcing mainstream media outlets to address topics—like conspiracy theories about Clinton's health—that they would otherwise ignore. (Schreckinger 2017)

The pro-Trump 4chan and Reddit communities tried to produce memes that would also appeal beyond the boards—to the public (the 'Normies'), by first testing them on Reddit before pushing them onto Twitter (Lukito 2019). The memes were then amplified by bots, creating a multi-platform disinformation campaign that actually led some people to believe that Hillary Clinton engaged in satanic rituals (spirit cooking meme) and was involved in a child-trafficking sex ring in the basement of a DC pizzeria (Pizzagate). While the grotesque nature of these memes could

---

fine themselves as unable to find a romantic or sexual partner despite desiring one. Incels are characterized by extreme misogyny, racism, resentment, and self-pity. The Southern Poverty Law Center describes them as "part of the online male supremacist ecosystem."

be seen as emblematic of carnival, especially misogynistic medievalesque accusations of witchcraft addressed to Hillary Clinton, they nonetheless led to real-life consequences, including an armed assault on the Comet Ping Pong pizzeria that does not even have a basement.

There are some indications that 4chan's support for Trump was at first caustic (Merrin 2019), with trolls enjoying the idea of supporting the election of a joke candidate for president—very much in line with the carnivalesque glorification of the carnival trickster-fool (Bakhtin 2015, p. 164). In carnival culture, the glorification, worship, and coronation of the king are done tongue-in-cheek. All the participants understand that the new 'king' is hardly up to the task in the real world. However, as the Trump campaign progressed, the trolls converged with the alt-right voices: "For a lot of people, on the first day it was like, 'This would be fucking hilarious,' and then when he started coming up with policy stuff—the border wall, the Muslim ban—people on the boards were like, 'This can't be real. This is the greatest troll of all time'" (Schreckinger 2017). 4chan's attitude towards Trump fits neatly into the carnival's perception of the trickster—he is, after all, "roi pour rire" (Bakhtin 2015), a "king for laughs"—almost literally the "lulz" motto of the trolling crowd. Moreover, focusing on the pleasure of laughter regardless of the hurt and damage it might cause is yet another hallmark of the carnivalesque discourse, where ideology is in plain sight of the alt-right mockery (May and Feldman 2019).

While the humanity of some of these Trump supporters may be questioned, others definitely possessed none at all. Bots, or software automatons, are involved in the creation, transmission, and controlled mutation of significant political messages over expansive social networks (Howard, Woolley, and Calo 2018). While bots, with their discursive power, had been harnessed in political communication for almost a decade (Ratkiewicz et al. 2011), only in the run-up to and in the aftermath of the 2016 election did bot hybrids become the focus of media and academic attention (Sindelar 2014; Pomerantsev and Weiss 2014; Thorsen 2018; Yan, Pegoraro, and Watanabe 2019; Keller and Klinger 2019). So-called Kremlin trolls are not 'classic' trolls identified in the literature who seek to aggravate users. Even though Kremlin trolls may ultimately provoke their targets emotionally, their main purpose is ideological, while regular trolls are usually devoid of ideology (Hardaker 2010). Kremlin trolls are real people who work in shifts for the Internet Research Agency, an organization allegedly under the control of late Russian oligarch, Yevgeny Prigozhin, reputed to have had close ties to President Putin (Bastos and Farkas 2019; Financial Times 2023). Their aim is to promote Kremlin-friendly discourse (Lukito 2019) while masquerading as 'organic' users. Both of these phenomena are quintessential simulacra, carnivalesque creatures who thrive in the setting of the carnival square—in the case of the Trump campaign, these were Reddit and Twitter users whose memes occasionally went beyond their PC-free world

into the mainstream discourse, often through Trump himself or his more prominent supporters.

The phenomenon of Internet trolls is a perfect embodiment the performance-
oriented culture of carnival, with their roots traced to Nordic folklore and trickster
culture (Buckels, Trapnell, and Paulhus 2014). As Quattrociocchi, Scala, and Sunstein (2016) note, the so-called 'echo-chambers' on social media reinforce selective
exposure and group polarization, further radicalizing the political debate that is
already polarized in the US (Westfall et al. 2015; McCarty, Poole, and Rosenthal
2016). With 62 % of American adults getting their news from social networks (Gottfried and Shearer 2016), many rely on social media for news coverage (Weeks and
Holbert 2013), as patterns of misinformation and their amplification via echo
chambers are becoming an everyday phenomenon.

While multidirectional discourse and social media in particular seemed to
have held a democratic promise, the anti-hierarchy nature of the carnival eventu-
ally led to other carnivalesque features becoming much more prominent in the
Trump campaign. It was the anti-establishment battle cry that principally appealed
to Trump voters (Berman 2016) but we should not forget about the main victims of
the carnival square - its abject.

Chapter 5: Displaced Abjection

"The cruelty is the point," the title of Adam Serwer's 2018 article in *The Atlantic* and of his 2021 book, is a pithy and illustrative catchphrase to describe Trump's campaign, presidency, and movement. It is immensely difficult to take stock of all of the callous decisions President Trump made, from a blanket ban on travel from some Muslim-majority nations and the separation of migrant children from their parents to neglecting victims of the COVID-19 pandemic. The kinds of racism that Trump trafficked are, of course, part and parcel of American politics rather than something he brought back to the field. Trump, however, made attacks on the dignity of the vulnerable a badge of pride. The cruelty did not stop when Trump left office in 2021. From the howling mob demanding the heads of Mike Pence and Nancy Pelosi to the transportation of refugees to Democrat-run cities orchestrated by Texas Governor Greg Abbott and Florida Governor Ron DeSantis: Trump showed the power of cruelty, and the GOP has since been enamored with it. For example, on September 15, 2022, Abbott sent a bus full of migrants to the Vice President's residence at the Naval Observatory in Washington DC—in response to comments Vice President Kamala Harris made on TV—using vulnerable, undocumented people as pawns in a publicity stunt to score political points with the GOP base and trigger the 'libs.'

The Trump carnival brings this cruelty to the fore, venerating it as a righteous form of transgression against an imagined oppression of political correctness, and in this case, the bogus argument that the Biden administration is pushing "open border" policies. This is a tradition for Trump, who enforced punitive policies towards communities of color before, during, and after his presidency (Abrajano and Hajnal 2015). Kivisto (2019), drawing on Shklar's warning about the fragile nature of liberal democracy (Shklar 2013) emphasized the gratuitous and strategic use of cruelty by the Trump administration while Giroux highlighted the additional cruel architecture of neoliberalism that reinforces white nationalism (Giroux 2019). However, the cruelty and the effort to further marginalize those who have been historically left outside of the power structures is in fact a constitutive element of the carnival. As Kallis notes, in a discussion on fascism (Kallis 2008), "the format of discharging violence created an exceptional psychological space where ritual transgression, and the anonymity of the crowd produced the illusion of an extraordinary experience of unbound permissibility, governed by the empathic lapse of conventional moral *norms*" (p. 6, emphasis added). In many ways, engaging in violence cements the group's identity against the perceived outsiders who are the targets of that violence. Using the concept of displaced abjection, this chapter discusses how the Trump carnival, populist as it is, is not focused on ridiculing or challenging elites, but instead *punching down*, by targeting marginalized groups. Through displaced abjection, we see how the Trump carnival is centered on licensing and encouraging transgressions against specific democratic norms that affirm human dignity and equality. Trump, by humiliating and insulting age-old enemies, translates what is broadly considered unacceptable and undemocratic behavior into a transgressive, carnivalesque politics of violating fundamental democratic norms of equality, dignity, and pluralism.

5.1 Displaced Abjection

Demonization is central to carnival culture. Bakhtin notes the presence in the carnivalesque tradition of "comic images of death" and "merry dilaniations" and argued that "laughter never conceals violence" or "builds pyres." This idealistic portrayal of the laughing culture is at odds with the many examples of the carnival's practice. Given its form as the transgression and violation of elite norms (the Church and the nobility, in this case), it is surprising that it was not the elites themselves that carnival culture demonized. Instead, carnival culture degrades a marginalized group, as in the case of Jews, as we mentioned in Chapter 3. This degradation of a targeted marginalized group is what we frame as "displaced abjection," in which the carnival protagonists focus their anger against someone who is lower than them in social hierarchy. Of course, the repetition of the image of a corrupt Hillary Clinton by Trump and his supporters is anti-elite and deeply sexist (and we dedicate the following chapter to this issue). Transgressions against the dignity and equality of those *truly* marginalized, with Trump's cruelty as an exemplar, play a crucial role in sustaining the carnival. The folk that reverses the hierarchy with the elite still keeps certain social groups on the very bottom of the social ladder who remain there through carnival practices of abuse. Thus, the effigy serves as the symbolic analogy of scapegoated groups and demonized 'Others.'

However, as Kelly points out (1990), the seemingly merry reversals of the carnival, with its comic violence, morphed into the grotesque of Stalin's terror that Bakhtin hints at. Stalin's purges were mass repressions often translated to a general public through the spectacle of show trials (Ellman 2001; Fitzpatrick 2018) with gruesome sentences being accompanied by laughter at the expense of the convicted "enemies of the people" (Groys 2017). Given that *Rabelais and His World* was written during the increasing repressions in the Soviet Union, with Bakhtin himself being exiled for his own work, dark allusions were all he could afford.

Abjection has been utilized in contemporary critical theory to describe how societies connote particular groups of people—mostly minority groups—as revolting figures (Tyler 2013). Some researchers also note that the pogrom violence of the

20th century also had a highly ritualistic and performative nature that was aimed at re-asserting the power that was perceived as threatened (Kallis 2007; Hagen 2005; Burke 2005). When we introduced abjection in Chapter 3, we developed on its theorization by Julia Kristeva in her famous 1982 book *Powers of Horror* (Kristeva 1982):

> The abject is not an ob-ject facing me, which I name or imagine. Nor is it an ob-jest, an otherness ceaselessly fleeing in a systematic quest of desire. What is abject is not my correlative, which, providing me with someone or something else as support, would allow me to be more or less detached and autonomous. The abject has only one quality of the object—that of being opposed to (p. 10).

At the same time, Kristeva pointedly gives agency to the abject as a challenge to the "master" (Kristeva 1982), often through its mere presence in the carnival. Its costumes exposed belly buttons and saggy breasts violating Renaissance norms that differentiated savagery and civilization. Further, modern abject art explores themes that transgress "our sense of cleanliness and propriety, particularly referencing the body and bodily function" (Ravenscroft and Gilchrist 2009). The mere presence of abjected and grotesque bodies signifies spaces of transgression in carnival, which we delve further into in Chapter 8.

Classifying someone as a subaltern is a performative move, often done by oppressors who claim the status of victims for themselves (Koplatadze 2019; Krystalli 2019, 2021). The affective narrative of victimization that tends to restructure communication (Chouliaraki 2021) prioritized Trump's rendering of America (and, more specifically, white men's in general) suffering at the hands of both domestic and foreign Others (Löfflmann 2022). Hence the "great again" slogan (Al-Ghazzi 2021): it's not only a call-back to a previous supposedly "great" man in presidential history, but also an implicit call to heal the vulnerability caused by those whom Trump and his campaign falsely represented as being in power. While a number of scholars have written on the politics of ressentiment in the Trump campaign and administration, Ganesh has a more apt term for this type of political grievance: white thymos, "the part of our souls that desires recognition of injustices done to us, draws our attention to the nexus of pride, rage, and indignation" (2020, pp. 893–894).

The grievances aired by Trump during his campaign were not new in the course of American history. While his constant blame game even earned him the title of Scapegoater-in-Chief (Heidt 2018), there is a definite political genealogy of right-wing politicians claiming unjustified victimhood from different societal groups and the government that are purportedly preventing the mainstream and privileged from continuing to bask in the same structural preferences. Especially on social media, the promise of violent fun at the expense of marginalized groups was a cheap means of empowerment in the capitalist media landscape (Anderson and Secor 2022). Apart from social media and mainstream media that were happy to report Trump's racist statements without proper contextualization, there were certain other outlets that thanks to Trump were propelled to the epicenter of the American media space. For instance, Breitbart cultivated the white victimhood narrative as well as anti-Black racism that propelled Trump's campaign (Inwood 2019).

In the American context there is another grim carnivalesque tradition—lynching. Lynching, marked by abnormal cruelty, crowds and publicity, continued as a violent tradition in the US peaking between 1890 and 1940 (Garland 2005). In many ways, lynchings were extremely carnivalesque as they also ultimately served to maintain the racial status quo. Lynching as a practice was foremost a spectacle (Jackson 2008) that was supposed to draw a public and let that public engage in the cruelty of very much pointedly placed abjection (Wood 2013). As Harold and DeLuca point out (2005), "images of the abject Jesus icon continue to be an indispensable focal point for Catholics. This corporeal spectacle serves as a testimony of an injustice ('look at what they've done to our Lord'), a warning of the risk of discipleship, and an ennobling of the martyr who sacrificed his or her life for others" (p. 275), which also led to Black communities in the US circulating the photographs of Emmett Till's body as proof of his vicious murder and to emphasize the grotesqueness of the violence as evidence of white racism (Harold and DeLuca 2005).

In the Trump carnival, displaced abjection is fundamentally about licensing the transgression of democratic norms. The Trump carnival's targets are racial, religious, and sexual minorities. If Trump started with "radical Islam" and "illegals," his carnival's effigies now include the as well "woke left" and non-binary people, all in the context of a narcissistic racial fantasy that imagines white Americans as those who are the truly oppressed, a narrative rendered in its most extreme form in theories of "white genocide" we discussed earlier in this book. Trump's radical cruelty towards immigrants and Muslims in particular, characteristic of his campaign and the counter-jihad social movements that supported it (see Pertwee 2020), is not only or simply racist. Trump's promises to ban all Muslims from entering the US or forcing Mexico to pay for a border wall are designed to transgress the red lines of democratic order itself: calling for blanket discrimination, a violation of the post-war civil rights tradition in the US, and claiming that his negotiating skills would make Mexico pay for a wall, certainly a non-starter in any serious diplomatic discussion, were intended to show that discrimination and bullying other countries signify strength and virtue.

In this sense, political correctness is a keyterm. On the right, use of the term 'political correctness' primarily refers to an oppressive silencing of free speech on the grounds of respecting the dignity and equality of others. In this regard, those who claim to be oppressed by political correctness lament that they are no longer entitled to offend others with full immunity from the consequences. This has played out in dramatic fashion in a galaxy of social media platforms, where far-right users (often those directly associated with fascist activism) are suspended or banned from platforms like Facebook and Twitter for violating these companies' rules and who then relocate to fringe platforms that provide unfettered, 'free speech' alternatives where there are few, if any, rules about offense. The 4chan board /pol/, an abbreviation of Politically Incorrect, celebrates the practice of transgressing politically correct discourse by purposefully causing offence, often with the goal of 'triggering' the libs. In making politically correct discourse—a set of norms that seek to enforce the dignity and equality of all groups in a public sphere—transgressive, the Trump carnival licenses hatred.

5.2 The Trump Carnival's Targets

Many commentators were quick to describe Trump as the carnival fool. Former New York City mayor Mike Bloomberg referred to him as a barking carnival clown (Smith 2020), while former Texas Governor Rick Perry described him as a carnival barking act (Dann 2015). Rodney Wallace Kennedy argues that Trump made every day a "Feast of Fools" (Kennedy 2021), connecting the temporary carnivalesque transgression to the white evangelicals' preference for the Trump campaign. In many ways, the entire presidential campaign was emblematic of "[the time turning] old power and truth into a carnival effigy, a funny monster that the people tormented with laughter in the square" (Bakhtin 2015, p. 101). The actual torment was reserved for somebody else. Despite its violation of 'high culture' and its heteroglossia, carnival preserves social hierarchy and ordering, rendering marginalized groups the focus of populist anger and frustration. The understanding that the hierarchy reversal and popular anger were play-pretend and not entirely real was a significant factor that was widely understood by the carnival crowd, hence the executions of the mock king and ritual abuse of groups that are in the minority and are unlikely to have a claim to power. This phenomenon is particularly visible in alt-right communities online, one of the main Trump supporting groups (Ganesh 2020).

Here, we cover the primary targets of the Trump carnival, identifying those groups that it renders into effigies against which transgressions are enacted. There is of course already an extensive literature on Trump's racism, his Islamophobia, the antisemites he tacitly supports, and the militant heteronormativity that characterizes right-wing politics today. Our aim in this chapter is not to rehash this well-known aspect of Trump's politics, but to show how displaced abjection functions as part of carnivalesque populism. For the Trump carnival, displaced abjection allows for the transgression of norms associated with the ceremonious elite and the manners of the so-called political establishment. By 'punching down,' the Trump carnival turns the derogation of minorities into a source of pride because it violates the democratic norms of diversity and equality. Displaced abjection in the Trump carnival is not simply the dehumanization of the other, it is about turning minorities into effigies that are nothing more than materials that serve as objects for transgression; respecting other humans becomes yet another taboo to violate. Fundamentally, while Trump's carnival is often seen as populist, it is not the elites that are transgressed against, but rather the rules and norms—of respect, dignity, equality, and the rule of law—with which they are associated (and it is well known that many of these elites have violated these norms).

There is a long tradition of dog-whistling rhetoric in American politics (Haney-López 2014), where coded racial appeals are supposed to cultivate resentment against non-white people. This tradition is also actively buttressed by the long tradition of racist humor (Pérez 2022), which will be examined futher in the laughing culture chapter. After all, despite Bakhtin's assertions, humor can also lead to abuse and violence. Moreover, many carnivalesque practices that are common on far-right platforms and social media are essentially echoes of blackface minstrel performances (Pérez 2022). Blackface minstrelsy refers to a form of entertainment that emerged in the United States in the early 19th century. It involved white performers darkening their skin with burnt cork or other substances to portray exaggerated caricatures of Black people. These performances were typically presented in theatrical shows, vaudeville acts, and later in early forms of media such as films and radio, not to mention early Disney cartoons. Many scholars consider blackface minstrelsy the first genuine American cultural product to be exported abroad (Thelwell 2020; Springhall 2008). Minstrel shows featured a variety of stereotypical portrayals of Black people, which were demeaning and offensive, reinforcing racial prejudices. The white performers would wear tattered clothing, apply exaggerated makeup, and engage in mocking behaviors to depict Black Americans as ignorant, lazy, and foolish. The shows often included songs, dances, comedic sketches, and jokes that perpetuated racial stereotypes (Saxton 1975). It was considered such a cultural mainstay that many new immigrants, even Jews, engaged in the practice (Rogin 1996). Blackface minstrelsy played a significant role in shaping popular culture in the United States during the 19th and early 20th centuries. It contributed to the normalization of racist attitudes towards and stereotypes of African Americans, perpetuating notions of inferiority and mockery, making characters such as Jim Crow, Mammy, Uncle Tom, or the 'uppity' black person trope, mainstays in American popular culture that are still common now (Lockett 2021). These performances were widely popular and reached audiences across different racial and social backgrounds and were a part of the carnival tradition in the US and Canada (Howard 2018; Lott 2013). The legacy of blackface minstrelsy is deeply intertwined with the history of racism and discrimination against Black people.

Another carnivalesque phenomenon that also has genealogical roots in minstrelsy is 'digital blackface,' a pervasive use of gifs on social media featuring Black people by non-Black people. The way Khadija Mbowe, a popular YouTuber, explains it, many popular reaction gifs exploit the same minstrelsy stereotypes but using contemporary Black entertainers and sportspeople as stand-ins. Moreover, Black people are treated as performers or masks through the decontextualized use of African-American Vernacular English (AAVE) and performative outrage by non-Black people about the perceived overuse of AAVE (Matamoros-Fernández 2020). Moreover, Kremlin trolls also engaged in blackface in order to cultivate a certain kind of Black identity on social media (Freelon et al. 2022), which exemplified the masked and carnivalesque nature of the global media ecology. Interestingly during his rallies, Trump appeared often much more 'politically correct' than on Twitter. In many cases, he let the opening speakers engage in more abjectionable rhetoric, often platforming Black conservative pundits, preachers, and performers. Diamond and Silk, also known as Lynette Hardaway and Rochelle Richardson, were an American conservative political commentary duo from the United States who often served as an opening act to Trump's rallies.

Perhaps one of the most evident forms of displaced abjection is summed up in the term 'illegals,' a vague appellation that Trump gives to those crossing the US's southern border. While this is only correlation, Google Trends showed a steady increase in the term 'illegals' in the aftermath of Trump's official presidential campaign announcement in June 2015 and peaked around the presidential elections in November 2016. 'Illegal,' like 'terrorist,' is a spectral term that comes to represent bodies crossing the southern border that are simultaneously racially other, criminal, and potential terrorists. In fact, as stories about "migrant caravans" came up during Trump's administration, on many occasions, he suggested that they were a route for so-called "radical Islam", and made frequent reference to the criminality of these so-called "illegals" (De Genova n.d.; Padilla 2022; Viladrich 2023), though it is important to note that Trump actually gained votes from Hispanic Texans and Floridians, which might be explained by reference not to physical attributes, but a dichotomy between legal, entrepreneurial immigrants and the spectral 'illegals' (Padilla 2022; Viladrich 2023).

As mentioned above, Donald Trump was one of the most prominent 'birthers'. Obama was born on August 4, 1961, in Honolulu, Hawaii. However, the birthers claimed that he was born in Kenya, his father's home country, and that his birth certificate was forged or non-existent. These claims were largely fueled by racial prejudice, xenophobia, and political opposition to Obama. Despite overwhelming evidence, including Obama's Hawaiian birth certificate and newspaper announcements of his birth in local Hawaiian newspapers from 1961, the birther movement persisted and gained some traction in conservative circles (Austin 2015). In April 2011, after years of speculation and demands from the birther movement, Obama released his long-form birth certificate. The document confirmed his birth in Hawaii and was certified as genuine by state officials. Despite this, a small group of die-hard birthers continued to promote this baseless conspiracy theory. This was more than poorly veiled racism: the fact that a Black man became the president was too much of a reversal of the status quo in American politics—to such an extent that Obama's election was widely viewed as evidence for the claim that racism has been overcome. In the logic of carnival, this reversal had to be corrected, with a return to the status quo of white men in power. Ultimately, the controversy did not gain widespread acceptance or have a significant impact on Obama's presidency, as he was reelected in 2012. However, it did highlight the power of conspiracy theories and the persistence of misinformation in public discourse, not to mention provided yet another opportunity for the mainstreaming of racist views.

At this stage of Trump's involvement in a presidential campaign, when he was not even a candidate, he already enabled very fringe voices. Moreover, Islamophobia became yet another major issue in the 2016 presidential campaign (Tesler 2018) following the call for "a complete and total shutdown of Muslims entering the United States" (Taylor 2015) proposed by Trump in the aftermath of the San Bernardino mass shooting. There is an immense literature on Islamophobia, and some recent research has pointed to Muslims being the most acutely affected of the targets of racial resentment, being seen as the "least-evolved" group in American society, even by other minority groups (Lajevardi and Oskooii 2018). There is also a long history of research into Islamophobia as part of a US empire and the subjection of Muslims to extensive systems of control and surveillance (Kumar 2012; Kundnani 2014; Massoumi, Mills, and Miller 2017). The literature on online hate speech, which focuses on the impacts on Muslim victims of hatred and abuse, Islamophobic networks often associated with Trump, and far-right movements, is also plentiful (Awan 2014; Berntzen 2019; Ekman 2015; Evolvi 2018; Poole et al. 2021; Vidgen and Yasseri 2020). Indeed, both Benkler, Faris, and Roberts (2018, p. 144) and Pertwee (2020) argue that Islamophobia was central to Trump's appeal, which of course built upon a much longer-term development of anti-Muslim groups in right-wing civil society (Bail 2014). As in many cases of abjection rhetoric, Islamophobic rhetoric did correlate with the rise of violence (Abdelkader 2016).

Antisemitism probably has one of the longest (displaced) abjection pedigrees to the extent that Jews were the focus of ritual carnivalesque abuse in the Middle Ages (Martin 2006; Bristol 2014). American politics and political communication has not been immune to antisemitic dog whistles or openly antisemitic remarks.

One of the main target of right-wing antisemitism is the figure of businessman and philanthropist George Soros, who has become one of the main targets of "Protocols of the Elders of Zion"-esque smears and harassment over the years, propagated by commentators ranging from Bill O'Reilly and Glenn Beck to Ron DeSantis (Langer 2022). In a sense, there is even some sort of continuity between Henry Ford, one of the main sponsors and spreaders of the Protocols conspiracy in the US, and Trump, another businessman who was trying to pin all his misfortunes on "Soros-sponsored" Deep State (Douglas 2020) and similar outrageous claims that his supporters actively spread (Bongino 2020). Especially after the 2022 and 2023 indictments, Trump doubled down on his antisemitic claims in his PAC and campaign emails. Moreover, Soros became yet another seemingly acceptable antisemitic dog whistle, with Republican candidates trading insults and accusations about which one of them is supposedly backed by Soros (Archive of Political Emails 2023; Beauchamp 2023). Even though Jewish space lasers have entered the mainstream discourse, some disillusioned Trump supporters have also moved to the right of Trump himself: hence, accusations of Trump running a MIGA campaign (Make Israel Great Again) or even himself being a Zion Don can be found on Reddit and 4chan (Luddy 2021).

While the 2016 campaign might seem relatively tame compared to the virulent transphobia and constant attacks on queer and trans rights of the 2020s, the queer community was far from safe from being a target of abuse. Trump himself did not necessarily make many homophobic or anti-queer statements, but he did significantly gut LGBTQ protections over the four years of his presidency. This kind of hypocritical attitude towards the queer community is illustrated by groups like "Gays for Trump" or other prominent gay, male, far-right figures such as Milo Yannopoulos (Tobin 2017). This provides a very good illustration of homonationalism, as an American gay identity was often used to buttress Trump's Islamophobia (Tobin 2017). If the far-right corners of the Internet that routinely traffic in homophobia in order to compensate for their fragile masculinity is somewhat understandable in this context, it was the Trump campaign that elevated many ultra-conservative pundits and politicians, who were previously only at the margins of the carnival square. If we take a look at the campaign ads of Ron DeSantis, he is very clearly targeting Trump's alleged ambiguity on LGBTQ+ rights by asserting that he is the true conservative who would strip away the remaining protections or even public visibility that the queer community still has.

Left-leaning political commentators and pundits are also not immune to homophobia. For starters, given the rather public displays of affinity between Trump and Russia's President Putin, the public on both sides of the Pacific Ocean did not hesitate to imagine the 'bromance' between Donald Trump and the Russian president. In the American case, this imaginary relationship brought increasingly hardcore pornographic references into the mainstream (Rowley 2017) that culminated in gay (slasher) romance fiction and an abundance of memes and other visual material on American social media. Archive of Our Own, one of the biggest fanfiction-hosting websites in the world to date, has 160 gay romance fan fiction stories featuring Trump and Putin. In the more mainstream spaces, in one his monologues Stephen Colbert on the *Late Show with Stephen Colbert*, emphatically thundered that "the only thing [President Trump's] mouth is good for is being Vladmir Putin's cockholster [censored]" (*The Late Show with Stephen Colbert* 2017). He later apologized for the statement, but the joke rather trafficked in homophobia than obscenity. Perhaps because of the obscenity (not the homophobia), this monologue was investigated by the Federal Communications Commission, but neither the host nor the network ended up being punished. Colbert did (sort of) apologize for the homophobic nature of the joke and made fun of the fact that the hashtag #FireColbert was trending on Twitter (Lopez 2017).

5.3 Practicing Displaced Abjection in the Trump Carnival

From referring to "shithole countries," and banning Muslims (Vitali, Hunt, and Thorp 2018), to his infamous 2020 tweet, "when the looting starts the shooting starts" (Sprunt 2020), Donald Trump uses racism, hatred, and bigotry to serve specific functions of transgression that direct the rage of his supporters. His use of displaced abjection is thus a powerful tool in violating norms of dignity, equality, and democracy. In the last section of this chapter, we walk through a few examples of how Trump practices displaced abjection. This is only a first set of examples. It is important to note that while we focus on misogyny, laughter, and sex and materiality in the chapters that follow, displaced abjection reappears throughout these carnivalesque practices that we describe in subsequent chapters.

It is deeply ironic that Trump—whose supporters are the first to cry when they feel their right to free speech is unjustly limited—would turn Colin Kaepernick into an effigy to score points. Following Kaepernick's insistence on kneeling during the national anthem to protest police brutality and racism—a protest that ultimately cost him his job as a quarterback for the San Francisco 49ers—and the movement of athletes that supported him, Donald Trump (as did many other conservatives) attempted to turn this into a weapon in the culture wars. In September 2017, Trump said of Kaepernick "Wouldn't you love to see one of these NFL owners, when somebody disrespects our flag, to say, 'Get that son of a bitch off the field right now. Out! He's fired. He's fired!'" (Graham 2017). This of course is not the only time during Trump's campaign that he singled out athletes. When Megan Rapinoe was asked if she would go to the White House if the

US women's soccer team she co-captained wins the World Cup, she responded, "I'm not going to the fucking White House." Donald Trump tweeted back, "Megan should WIN before she TALKS!" (North 2019). Both Kaepernick and Rapinoe are politically outspoken against Trump and the far-right politics he represents: Kaepernick, a model for Black activism fighting against police brutality and racism; and Rapinoe, who herself took a knee during the anthem before doing so was banned by the US Soccer Federation, who has been outspoken about her sexuality. In both cases, attacking these athletes is a way for Trump to stir up cultural polarization to reinforce his appeal to his base.

One of the most racist and publicized incidents of the Trump administration took place in January 2018, during a meeting on immigration. According to several sources, including lawmakers who were present at the meeting, lawmakers were discussing protections for immigrants from countries affected by political unrest and economic challenges. It was reported that when discussing immigrants from Haiti, El Salvador, and African countries, Trump allegedly asked, "Why are we having all these people from shithole countries come here?" (Dawsey 2018). This comment is a quintessential example of the carnivalesque abject in Trumpspeak. As Bahrainwala (2021) notes, the statement "locates this racism on the axis of toileting, and ties it to both anatomy and infrastructure since 'shitholes' can be interpreted as one's anus or as unplumbed, squatting toilets," as contamination is an inextricable part of the abject. The previous, seemingly politer version of this idea was the "drain the swamp" slogan, a fascist slogan that combined the notion of dirt and the act of purification performed by the populist leader. In this way, dog whistling became a technology of abjection: by technically not breaking 'the norms' of political correctness, Trump and his supporters signaled the transgressiveness of their rhetoric. Even though Trump, throughout his campaign, did not shy away from using openly racist rhetoric or from openly accusing certain ethnic groups of "bringing drugs and crime," he did not necessarily need to specify who it was doing that. For that, he needed to keep repeating his "build the wall" chant, which was supposed to instantly remind his audience and the media of who it was he wanted to protect the people from. Emphasizing the fact that Mexico was supposed to be paying for the wall only elevated the whistle to bullhorn.

Trump's presidential campaign and his presidency had a significant effect on the mainstreaming of far-right rhetoric as well as conspiracy theories (Bleakley 2023). One of the most prominent ones, the aforementioned Pizzagate, ended up in gun violence that could have turned deadly. The conspiracy theory, which emerged from within the alt-right Twitter community, alleged that John Podesta's emails exposed some members of the Democratic party as being part of a DC pizzeria-based child-sex ring (Bleakley 2023; Kang 2016). The theory gained momentum primarily through social media platforms (Fisher, Cox, and Hermann 2016).

Supporters of Pizzagate pointed to supposed coded language and symbols found in the leaked emails, claiming they contained hidden references to illegal activities. The allegations were thoroughly investigated and debunked by law enforcement agencies, journalists, and independent researchers. Despite the lack of evidence, the conspiracy theory had real-world consequences. In December 2016, an individual motivated by Pizzagate beliefs entered Comet Ping Pong with a firearm, firing shots but causing no injuries. As children are seen universally as symbols of the future, attacks on them can be viewed as an existential threat to a nation. This is also the way homophobic fears are stoked: in the US, and most recently in Russia, homosexuality has constantly been discursively linked to pedophilia (Alcoff 1996; Gaufman 2017). This is the mechanism borne out of 'blood libel' cases, which were pretexts for organizing Jewish pogroms: false rumors about 'killing of babies' and the 'use of their blood' during Passover is a perfect way to incite hatred.

Hillary "nasty woman" Clinton is also present in the blood libel narrative. Trump's constant engagement with antisemitism, in which he or his surrogates have implied that Hillary Clinton had some mysterious ties with "Jewish capital"—such as the "History made" poster with the $100 bills and Star of David image, or his last campaign ad, which was universally condemned as antisemitic (Rozsa 2016)—sustained this incredibly old anti-feminist trope with its antisemitic tinge. Long after the presidential campaign and presidency, in his post-indictment in the classified documents case speech Trump stated: "Together we stand up to the globalists, we stand up to the Marxists. [...] We stand up to the open border fanatics and [...] the lawless prosecutors [...] in blue states" (CJ 2023). Much as Nixon used "heroin" and "marijuana" to signify Blacks and hippies, Trump signifies the Democratic party with antisemitic dog whistles.

While the US is known for its racist practices of law enforcement and frequent reports of police shootings of unarmed Black men, the country reached a new low on May 25, 2020 in Minnesota. On that day, Minneapolis police officers responded to a call about allegedly passing a forged banknote at a convenience store. George Floyd was arrested by four officers, namely Derek Chauvin, Thomas Lane, J. Alexander Kueng, and Tou Thao. During the arrest, Officer Chauvin knelt on Floyd's neck for an extended period, even as Floyd pleaded for his life, saying, "I can't breathe." Floyd's pleas were captured on video by a bystander, and the footage quickly circulated on social media, generating outrage. The video showed Floyd being held down on the ground, face-first, while Chauvin knelt on his neck for over nine minutes. Floyd became unresponsive and was later pronounced dead at a nearby hospital. The incident raised concerns about the excessive use of force and the mistreatment of Black individuals by law enforcement officers. Following the release of the video, protests erupted in Minneapolis and soon spread to other cities across the United States and around the world. The demonstrations called for justice for George Floyd, an end to police brutality, and an examination of systemic racism within the criminal justice system. The Black Lives Matter movement sought to raise awareness about the disproportionate use of force against black individuals and to advocate for meaningful change in policing and racial equality. Many conservative commentators, instead of condemning the murder, focused on Mr. Floyd's background, as though any rumors of substance abuse could ever excuse police brutality. This tendency highlighted the fact that the pro-Trump crowd saw a threat in the actual carnivalesque resistance and reversal of the Black Lives Matter (BLM) movement: Trump's carnival sought to conserve the existing hierarchy that the BLM movement questioned. During the protests, Trump tweeted, "When the looting starts the shooting starts" (Sprunt 2020), a phrase that was originally used in the summer of 1967 in the context of racial riots in Miami. This, once again from the president that referred to those marching among white supremacists in Charlottesville as "fine people," was a strategic transgression against the right to protest, using age-old myths of Black people as violent rioters. Trump's post was too extreme even for Facebook, which led to his account being suspended by the platform.

The COVID-19 pandemic provided yet another example of how carnivalesque politics can incorporate experts in processes of displaced abjection. With the carnivalesque reversal of the hierarchy, a complete disregard for authority and expertise makes complete sense. Why would you want to go to a pharmacy when the quack doctor next door (or podcast) is selling his wonder potion, as members of the alternative influence network like Alex Jones did? Who cares if ivermectin is for horses when the influencers say it works and is being deliberately covered up by the health institutions? In this case, Antony Fauci, one of the main faces of governmental expertise, became the target of so many violent threats that he was forced to live under police protection. The main enemy in carnival is the enemy of freedom, consequently slogans abounded among the anti-vax and anti-lockdown crowds who demanded to get a haircut, to not be "muzzled," and to not be "injected with poison." They even compared themselves to Jews for the "repressions" they faced because of their anti-science attitudes. Again, the notion of freedom, so important in the American context, was stretched to the extreme with the wide-ranging protests against lockdowns, mask mandates, and vaccines. The attempts by social media to dampen the spread of misinformation only led to the emergence of online communities that used coded language that would not get them into trouble.

Displaced abjection is a central feature of the carnival, but it should not be understood simply as racism. It is a complex process that incorporates a multitude of different actors and models that serve as the objects at whose expense transgression takes place. This derogation and dehumanization of the 'Other' is about violating fundamental norms as such, about transgressing against the basic values of democracy. With such displaced abjection, Trump manages to render hatred a populist act of reclaiming power. This happens through the identification of specific targets, projected as specters in the case of 'illegals' and 'radical Islam,' while still drawing on older, masked forms of racism and antisemitism. After all, the participants at the "Unite the Right" rally in Charlottesville in June 2017 that featured Neo-Nazis, Ku Klux Klan, "alt-right" and neo-Confederates among others chanted "Jews will not replace us" and other racist slogans. Trump, of course, said there were "very fine people on both sides", referring both to counter-protestors and the white supremacists at the rally. Trump tacitly condoned these extremists, and his administration pandered to their hateful, violent, and anti-democratic beliefs. We argue that displaced abjection in the Trump carnival also makes use of many different targets, from athletes standing up against injustices to experts like Dr. Fauci during the pandemic. As we move to three practices of carnival in the final parts of this book, we discuss how multidirectionality, displaced abjection, and carnivalesque populism come together in the transgressive, but ultimately anti-democratic, practices of laughing, misogyny, sex and materiality in the Trump carnival.

Chapter 6: Laughing Culture

"Foul-mouthed, crafty, ugly, violent, happy." This is not a description of Donald Trump, although it could have been uttered by one of his critics, but rather a character in a Russian fairground performance staple—Petrushka, a hooked nose and hunchbacked puppet clown (Kelly 1990). According to Catriona Kelly, Petrushka is a perfect foil for the subversive, grotesque, and ambivalent carnival of Mikhail Bakhtin as this character from Russian fairgrounds was able to engage in profanity, obscene acts, and grotesquery. Petrushka is a mask himself, allowing the puppetmaster to air their own grievances in a obscene way. The investigation of the laughing culture of the Middle Ages and the Renaissance was Bakhtin's primary aim in his study that defined carnival culture (Bakhtin 2015). Moreover, Bakhtin pushed against the "crude modernizing" interpretation of the people's laughing culture as inherently negative satirical laughter and idealized even the carnivalesque obscenities as "sparks of a single carnival fire that renews the world" (Bakhtin 2015, p. 12). This point of view earned him quite a bit of criticism from later authors who were wary of Mikhail Mikhailovich characterizing the Middle Ages as a time of carefree merriment, despite the intellectual potential of carnival as a theoretical framework (Boyarskaya 2015).

It is obvious that Bakhtin saw laughing culture as the most interesting part of the carnivalesque. He was primarily inspired by the Ukrainian writer Nikolai Gogol's satire, where

> the word of laughter is constructed by Gogol in such a way that its goal is not a simple indication of individual negative phenomena, but the opening of a special aspect of the world as a whole. In this sense, Gogol's zone of laughter becomes a zone of contact. Here the contradictory and incompatible are united, come to life as a connection. (Bakhtin 2005, p. 183)

It is that zone of contact and connection to the more folkloric forms of laughter, parody, and satire that was significant and by definition anti-authoritarian for Bakhtin (Pan'kov 2010). Exploring folkloric laughter was his main idea and motivation for the study of Rabelais in the first place. He idealized the notion of folkloric laughter as an anti-authoritarian force and many theorists followed his lead. Carl Lindahl, for instance, in his "Bakhtin's Carnival Laughter and the Cajun Country Mardi Gras" (1996), argues that the core carnival primary mode is parody that targets "the ossified culture of the elite" (p. 57). As humor is often seen as "the enjoyment of incongruity" (Tsakona and Popa 2011, p. 11), it becomes vital to the carnivalesque culture, where enjoyment is central and laughing is its marker. Political humor then becomes "a communicative resource spotting, highlighting, and attacking incongruities originating in political discourse and action" (Tsakona and Popa

2011, p. 6). The latter observation has become particularly vital in American late-night comedy and satire, where highlighting hypocrisy among liberal or conservative politicians has become a whole genre (Peterson 2008; Samoilenko et al. 2016).

In terms of humor, research confirms the lack of hierarchy reversal as well. Especially research dealing with racism and Islamophobia shows that asymmetries among countries as well as (Western) racial hierarchies are reflected in humorous depictions that are supposed to be subversive (Cotter 2014; Malmqvist 2015). In other words, skits, cartoons, and caricatures might mock certain personalities, but they still preserve a racial or geopolitical hierarchy as exemplified by instances of misogynoir (Razack and Joseph 2021) or portrayals of Russia or the Arab Spring (Purcell, Heitmeier, and Van Wyhe 2017). As Raul Pérez notes, racist humor has been used as a mechanism for social cohesion in the US where the cohesion of the white dominant social groups was ensured at the expense of the non-white ones (Pérez 2022).

The widely praised Soviet political joke, *the anekdot*, was indeed one of the rare discursive spaces of ambivalence and hierarchy reversal, in which powerless Soviet citizens could make fun of the political system (Graham 2003). Many authors theorized humor in the Soviet Union as a mode of hegemonic control (Minchenia, Törnquist-Plewa, and Yurchuk 2018), especially through its state-sponsored forms (Klumbyte 2012). However, in the same breath, this space of ambivalence offered room for ethnic jokes extolling racist stereotypes and prejudice against indigenous groups such as Chukchi or other racialized ethnic groups (Laineste 2008). Laughing at the regime took place, but the laughing culture still treated some more equally than others. Thus, humor served to support and strengthen the existing social order, even when occasionally used for dissent (Pearce and Hajizada 2014). Most importantly, humor that ridicules ethnic minorities as inferior or dangerous makes them an object of symbolic violence (Pérez and Ward 2019) or, in our framework, displaced abjection.

Humor is a powerful tool and laughing culture (often not named as such, but instead termed satire or humor) has become a vital part of populist communication (Wagner and Schwarzenegger 2020; Sienkiewicz and Marx 2022). Many politicians are afraid of coming off as ridiculous or of being ridiculed. Being the butt of late-night comedians' jokes can be career-ending in the American context (Farnsworth and Lichter 2019). At the same time, humor can serve as a very powerful mechanism for the normalization of offensive rhetoric (Wodak 2020; Wodak, Culpeper, and Semino 2021). But the important question is who is making fun of whom and what kinds of jokes are being made? Michael Billig (2005) emphasized that humor is often indicative of social hierarchies that are not easily reversed in the ambivalent humorous space. Late-night comedians in this respect have a name and do not necessarily represent anonymous humor from below (Kuipers 2008).

While late-night comedians do often 'punch up,' it is the more anonymous, grass roots humor that would be considered more Bakhtinian. However, on the grass roots level, "[u]sers appear to gain benefits from participating in a community and jointly making fun of outgroups, which might further strengthen the ties to extreme right positions" (Schwarzenegger and Wagner 2018).

Bakhtin argued that "peculiar folk humor" never merged with the official culture of the ruling classes (Bakhtin 2015), because popular culture was hostile to high culture. It is possible to contend that, through the multidirectional nature of Trump's digital carnival, this merger became possible. Even though some of the more obscene iterations of the humor—for instance, Stephen Colbert's cock-holster tirade (mentioned above in Chapter 5: "Displaced Abjection") or Samantha Bee's "feckless cunt" backlash (discussed below in Chapter 7: "Misogyny")—were somewhat sanctioned, but nevertheless became relatively mainstream. One of the more conventional types of Trump parody—Alec Baldwin's Trump impression that featured relatively lifelike facial prosthetics, gesturing, and speech—was extremely popular, with skits featuring him garnering up to 30 million views on You-Tube alone. Trump's constant criticism of *Saturday Night Live* (SNL) skits that featured Baldwin impressions also made SNL a much more relevant voice in the heteroglot US discourse. Obviously, as an example of the perceived 'liberal type' of humor, it was not necessarily widely viewed or discussed among the more right-wing-leaning electorate, but Trump managed, through his accusation of media bias, to use SNL to his strategic advantage (Becker 2020) by inoculating viewers against Baldwin's anti-Trump satire. Nonetheless, Trump even hosted SNL in November 2015, claiming "part of the reason I am here is that I know how to take a joke. They have done so much to ridicule me over the years, this show has been a disaster for me."[8] He was then joined by Taran Killam as Donald Trump and Darrell Hammond as Donald Trump. However, when comedian Larry David shouted out from the audience "Trump is a racist," the audience laughed at it. David explained that he was paid money to say that. Another issue is that even edited volumes on late-night comedy and humor during the Trump era do not necessarily feature or even include in their datasets right-wing comedy shows (Farnsworth and Lichter 2019; Young 2019), apart from more recent books that deal directly with this academic lacuna (Sienkiewicz and Marx 2022) and emphasize how irony was exploited by the far right to normalize their racist and misogynist content (Woods and Hahner 2019).

---

8 https://www.youtube.com/watch?v=PkLzSLkYnGc.

6.1 Conservative and Far-Right Laughter

So how did laughing culture become so central to American politics? Rod Hart (2013) would argue that the satire or at least the type of satire that *The Daily Show* embraced with Jon Stewart, while being an important part of political communication in the early 2000s, contributed to the depoliticization of the American electorate. Dannagal Young (2019) argues that a conservative/liberal divide in American politics translates into a type of laughing culture divide as well and suggests that a conservative mode of comedy is outrage. However, Bauer (2023), and by extension Sienkewicz and Marx and Pérez, would disagree and point to the scholarly neglect of conservative and racist humor. Paradoxically, the Bakhtinian juxtaposition between high and low culture was somehow translated into cultural capital for liberals, who are supposedly the only funny ones (Sienkiewicz and Marx 2022). If we follow Sienkiewicz and Marx (2022), laughter becomes a type of mainstreaming mechanism, where humor conceals nationalism (Topinka 2018) and provides an affective release associated with feelings of superiority over others (Boxman-Shabtai and Shifman 2014). In this way, laughter becomes a form of joy that comes from transgressing the norms of decency—arguably what laughing culture (and carnival) has always done (Stevens 2007).

Laughter is often associated with the grotesque: not just in Bakhtin's work, but in more modern interpretations that situate the grotesque somewhere between the comic and the terrifying (Thomson 2017), even though in the Rabelaisian tradition laughter and the grotesque were inextricably linked (Saddik 2012). This is because of the laughter that the grotesque is supposed to produce, by any means. Even Trump's leadership style can be described as grotesque from an aesthetic perspective (Taylor 2018), something to be experienced from an affective point of view. By being both a laughingstock and a court jester—or, as Mike Bloomberg would say, "a carnival barking clown," Trump became part of the attraction that is also immune to the laughing critique of the 'normies.' After all, in American culture, people who work at the 'carnival' (carnies) are frequently stereotyped as free spirits that are not beholden to the norms of society, relationships, or the state (Truzzi and Easto 1972), a type of peripatetic ethos that is marked by transgression (Kirby 2004). By partaking in the Trump carnival and the laughing culture of the Trump campaign, its critics embraced the laughing culture themselves, but without the claims to (carnie) authenticity that Trump himself could assert (Lacatus and Meibauer 2022). Moreover, Trump's own supporters embraced the left-wing mockery by appropriating the meme "Orange man bad" to point out the lack of criticism of Trump's policies as opposed to his physical attributes (Danesi 2022).

At the same time, Hillary Clinton's attempts to partake in the laughing culture were often rebuked and seen as inauthentic (Kolehmainen 2017), especially by online audiences (Davis, Love, and Killen 2018). How did regular people view the candidates? According to the findings of Moody-Ramirez and Church (2019), Clinton-meme pages were more likely to focus on her email scandal and wealth, while those featuring Trump focused on his campaign promises and physical appearance—often emphasizing his hairdo, physical features, and skin tone. The authors claim that their findings disprove the importance of gender in the election campaign, but the results definitely confirm the importance of carnival in the campaign: focus on the materiality of Trump and the critique of Clinton's elite status are extremely relevant here.

As mentioned above, Bakhtin was overly optimistic about the nature of laughter and its positive effects. At the same time, he quotes Julian Kayser, saying, "Laughter mixed with bitterness at the transition to the grotesque takes on the features of mocking, cynical and, finally, satanic laughter" (quoted in Bakhtin 2015, p. 33). Satanic laughter is definitely not something benevolent, even in Bakhtin's interpretation, and with the carnival being a representation of hell, he found ways to extract its benevolent features (Bakhtin, quoted in Lock 1991):

> If the Christian hell devalued earth and drew men away from it, the carnivalesque hell affirmed earth and its lower stratum as the fertile womb, where death meets birth and a new life springs forth (p. 78).

This type of satanic laughter is best exemplified by the subreddit r/ImGoingToHell-ForThis. Robert Topinka points out that because of its supposedly satiric and participatory nature, it's a carnivalesque space. Even its name—I'm going to hell for this—is carnivalesque, as carnival is supposed to signify hell in the first place. Topinka argues, then, that this subreddit presents a different version of a "cloaked" website, one in which the obviousness of the cloak does not staunch the proliferation of racism and nationalism (Topinka 2018). What users do is target the perceived force of political correctness by repurposing and remixing traditional media images in ways that violate the terms of political correctness. Thus, it might fly under the radar as 'humor' but it is yet another manifestation of racism and white supremacy in the guise of joking. No wonder Trump T-shirts are often categorized as "Funny" or "Humorous" on Amazon, even if they have literal hate speech on them.

WWE (World Wrestling Entertainment) and its annual professional wrestling event WrestleMania are often accused of being part of low "(white) trash" culture (Mathewson 2018). It is one of the largest and most popular wrestling events in the world, featuring high-profile matches, celebrity appearances, and extravagant budgets. The tournament is known for its spectacle, combining athleticism, storytelling, and entertainment, so it is no wonder it has also been analyzed through a

Bakhtinian lens (Canella 2016). Over the years, WrestleMania has become a pop culture phenomenon, featuring guest appearances by celebrities from the worlds of sports, entertainment, and music. The event often includes musical performances, special entrances, and elaborate sets and stages.

WWE represents a very American version of carnival with its laughing culture, play-pretend, extreme commercialization, gluttonous enjoyment and spectacle of bodies. Moreover, WrestleMania has been singled out as one of the modes through which to understand Trump's diplomacy (Day and Wedderburn 2022) or modus operandi (Moon 2022; Mendes 2016). Not only did Trump develop his own persona in the context of WrestleMania (Hall, Goldstein, and Ingram 2016), but, as David Moon (2022) specifically addresses, Trump used WWE tricks in his presidential campaign, especially the performativity and stage nature of some of the abuse and the temporality of the event. This was supposed to bode well for his presidential campaign.

On July 2, 2017, Donald Trump, as President of the United States tweeted a violent doctored video of himself punching somebody whose head was replaced with a CNN logo. The video and subsequent memes originated during WrestleMania 23, which took place on April 1, 2007. In a scripted storyline, he participated in a "Battle of the Billionaires" match alongside WWE chairman Vince McMahon. During the match, Trump tackled McMahon and delivered a series of staged punches. This moment from WrestleMania 23 was later edited and repurposed by Internet users to create the Trump punching meme. The images or videos were manipulated to show Trump throwing punches at various targets, often accompanied by humorous or satirical captions. The meme became popular on social media platforms, particularly on Twitter, where users would share edited versions of the original footage, replacing the CNN logo with the logos or heads of other people that they saw as hostile to Donald Trump. However, in his position as President this meme can no longer be seen as just a joke.

6.2 Late-Night Shows

When Trump descended the Trump Tower escalator to announce his presidential campaign, most late-night comedy show hosts were jubilant. Seth Meyers credited Trump's entire presidential campaign on his own performance at the White House Correspondents' Dinner, where he spent a considerable amount of time mocking Trump, who was in the audience. It is possible that yet another routine at the White House Correspondents' Dinner also had an effect—that of Barack Obama. Jon Stewart, John Oliver and others were also excited about Trump's run because of the amount of comedic material it would provide. The transition at *The Daily*

Show from host Jon Stewart to Trevor Noah was also in part enabled by the abundance of material inspired by the Trump campaign, despite the initial struggles suffered by the transition (Cuccinello 2016). It is important to note that by 2015, a tectonic change in the late-night show landscape had taken place, with many older comedians retiring and being replaced by younger personalities, with eleven shows on offer, seven of them airing almost daily (Baumgartner 2017). As Steven Farnsworth and Robert Lichter note,

> [The] growing aggressiveness of late night comedians is also occurring in a media environment that expands the attention they receive. Market forces encourage the comics to do so when traditional news outlets connect with smaller and more partisan audiences, when growing numbers of news consumers want their media diet to be highly entertaining, and as the boundaries between news and satire have become increasingly blurred. (Farnsworth and Lichter 2019, p. 10)

In fact, it is because of the centrality of the laughable aspect of the Trump campaign (Waisanen 2019) and the expanded transgressive nature of the conservative laughter (Smith 2018; Webber et al. 2021) that the carnivalesque metamorphosis of politics took place. Moreover, Danesi (2022) argues that Trump's campaign and presidency had a transformative effect on the American comedic tradition. He examines a plethora of genres and claims that the mocking of Trump was less effective as a political strategy in part due to the latter's experience in the entertainment industry. Crediting Bakhtin and one of the authors of this book, Danesi explores specifically Trump's role as a profane mocker, "a blend of commedia dell'arte personage, Archie Bunker redux, and P. T. Barnum hustler, who understood the power of humor to sway minds" (p. 1), and his role in delineating the laughing spaces between the political parties. According to Bakhtin, laughter is supposed to unite, but, in the Trump carnival, it divides.

Meier notes that the carnivalesque turn in American politics led to a change in late-night show politics as well. Using the example of Stephen Colbert's show he argues that Colbert employed "his carnivalesque capacity to discipline the president for abdicating the rhetorical and political norms of the presidency" (Meier 2020, p. 9). Trump himself, in a moment of shrewd political analysis, correctly observed: "[There's nothing funny about what he says. And what he says is filthy. And you have kids watching] And it only builds up my base. It only helps me, people like him" (Trump, quoted in Meier 2020). Of course, Trump fails to mention that whatever he says himself is not necessarily funny for the other side either, but it is not Democrat voters that he is addressing and his oxymoronic trickstery makes him immune from most barbs while boosting media ratings that live off them. As journalists Jethro Nededog and Skye Gould (2017) point out, "[Colbert's] decision to go harder on politics instead of ignoring his 'Colbert Report' roots, led by a new showrunner brought on last year, seems to have been a good one. Colbert's audience grew 13%," whereas Fallon—who previously posted the best ratings in the time-slot—"lost about 17% of his audience between the 2015–2016 and 2016–2017 seasons." Political comedy is a big business after all.

Chapter 7: Misogyny

7.1 Carnivalesque Misogyny

According to Bakhtin, carnival culture is inherently woman-phobic. If in the Gallic and mythical tradition men are supposed to be more fearful of their sons who might come to kill them and take their position in society or their throne—from Zeus and his daddy Chronos to Oedipus and King Laius (Bakhtin 2015)—in the carnival this fear is projected onto the woman who actually gives birth to the said son (Bakhtin 2015, p. 110). The fear is then projected onto women's genitals as the place where the threat is supposed to originate—the "pussy" that Trump claimed to brazenly "grab." Bakhtin himself connects this carnivalesque fear to the "fear of change and renewal [which] here appears in [the] form of fear of the horns [i. e., the fear of female infidelity, being cuckolded], of the betrothed, of the fate embodied in the image [of] woman who puts to death the old and gives birth to the new and the young" (Bakhtin 2015, p. 110). This type of fear still exists in Bakhtin's native Russian language: one of the worst situations in which one can find oneself in is described through the obscene term for women's genitals. In the ancient Slavic pagan culture that associated Mother Earth with a woman, the curse of death on someone was literally to send someone to the place from whence they were born—woman's crotch.

In carnivalesque iconography, especially in the Middle Ages, women's physical attributes played a major role (Kolyazin 2002). The full-body costumes—masks—depicted in the *Schoenbartbuch*, a very meticulous graphic illustration of the carnival in Nuremberg (*Schembartlauf*), featured several common characters, for instance, "demon with a bird head" or "a savage woman" that had exposed breasts, not to mention a mainstay of the procession—"an old hag" that would carry a bucket with a female doll that was supposed to indicate the sinful lust of the medieval bath houses. It is not surprising that it was the women who served as avatars of and were blamed for promiscuity (Leonardo and Chrisler 1992), not to mention being impugned for the spread of sexually transmitted diseases (Gilman 2019). This all fits very well with the folkloric tales of women with toothy vaginas trying to find and emasculate men during intercourse (Gaufman 2022) or at the very least give them a nasty venereal souvenir.

As a number of researchers have pointed out, Bakhtin is comparatively silent on the topic of gender (Barta et al. 2013; Ginsburg 1993), apart from pointing out the carnivalesque praise of the fertile feminine body that usually led to misogynistic satire (Byrd 1987). This is in stark contrast to the more recent (postcolonial) literature on carnival that specifically emphasized the gender-bending aspect of the practice (Cowan 1994; Outar 2017). At the same time, the perception of the female body was sometimes interpreted as "unruly resistance to a monologizing and specularizing discourse of phallic authority" (Nell 2001). Despite carnival's emancipatory promise for women, it was still infamous for its portrayal of "senile, pregnant hags" (Russo 1986) that were supposed to symbolize the idea of rebirth. Ultimately, it did not offer a complete inversion of the male/female hierarchy as the taboos were re-deployed in an ambivalent way and it was specifically the (grotesque) female body that became the main subject of derision and laughter (Russo 1986). The term 'hag' has been used to such an extent to shame women online that it led, in a very Bakhtinian spirit of reversal, to feminist appropriation of these appellations (Sundén and Paasonen 2018): "[the] feminist comedic universe [is] densely populated by woman-splainers, woman-spreaders, cuntblockers, absent mothers, female stalkers, middle-aged women with a taste for fresh meat, lesbophobia, old-girls-networks, and the occasional 'good' meninist girl."

Misogynistic practices related to carnival are ubiquitous and the digital ecosystem has facilitated online flows of misogyny in numerous ways. Sarah Sobieraj (2018) noted in the aftermath of the Trump campaign how women being driven out of digital spaces through at least three strategies, whereby online harassers intimidate, use femininity to undermine women's contributions, and call attention to physicality. Indeed, digital misogyny should be viewed "not merely as a feeling, attitude or type of behaviour towards women but rather as a method or set of methods that are used—whether deliberately or subconsciously—to keep women 'in their place'" (Ging and Siapera 2019, p. 2). The trend for digital misogyny was best exemplified by the Gamergate and "the fappening" online anti-feminist actions (Massanari 2017), where in the first case women and minority gamers and game developers were systematically harassed; and in the second, nude photos of female celebrities were acquired and shared via different platforms. There is a lot of evidence that both of these events were heavily motivated by revenge fantasies and geek masculinity that was further enabled by the toxic technoculture of online platforms (Banet-Weiser and Bratich 2019).

7.2 Trump's Misogyny

It is not surprising, then, that a lot of Trump and far-right anxiety is connected to women's behavior and femininity altogether. Several scholars have connected the Gamergate scandal (Merrin 2019) to one of the proto-Trumpian publics that emerged before the full-blown 2016 presidential elections actually took place. Moreover, the fear of emasculation is so mainstream that even Trump's critics were obsessed with exposing Trump as less of a man (Kelly 2018; Smirnova

2018) and maintaining a certain gendered ideal of masculinity. Thus, even the idea of presenting Trump as the "toddler in chief" (Drezner 2020; Klikauer and Campbell 2020) or depicting him in diapers were essentially links in the same misogynistic train of thought. After all, accusations of "toddler tantrums" are essentially the same feminization technique that presupposes a rational male body as the norm versus an emotional, often female, body of the other (Jimenez 1997; Ussher 2013). By flying giant Trump baby blimps dressed in diapers or erecting naked statues of him with small penises, his opponents effectively reinforced a gendered hierarchy.

As Kelly Wilz points out (2016), the double standards of treating female politicians in the 2016 elections were on full display, where voices, appearances and demeanor of female presidential candidates were constantly criticized. Serial misogynists and abusers in the newsrooms (Poniewozik and Lyons 2017) often broadcast a politer version of what one could find on social media, with Donald Trump actively mainstreaming this type of discourse. *Saturday Night Live* highlighted Trump's misogyny in their cold open about the final presidential debate in October 2016 when Alec Baldwin as Trump proceeded to claim that "no one has more respect for women."[9] The entire planet erupted into laughter at the deceit of this statement.

Another side of the carnival that we highlighted in previous chapters is related to the different types of voices that are heard. Trump himself sought to elevate more marginal ones that were not necessarily a part of the general discourse. One of the most effective platforms for him was, of course, Twitter, where he routinely re-tweeted accounts with very few followers as long as their posts resonated with his agenda. Trump was infamous for his misogyny even before the elections, routinely referring to women he did not like as dogs (Graham 2020; Boatright and Sperling 2019) One of many such cases occurred when Trump retweeted a meme that featured an unflattering picture of Ted Cruz's wife—at that point Ted Cruz was competing against Trump in the Republican primaries. The retweet featured a split-screen image with an unflattering photo of Heidi Cruz alongside a glamorous photo of Melania Trump. The tweet was captioned, "A picture is worth a thousand words." The retweet drew criticism and sparked controversy, with many people considering it an inappropriate and personal attack on Heidi Cruz, but entirely unsurprising in the American misogynistic context where women's physical attributes are used in political argumentation (Sobieraj 2018).

The incident led to a heated exchange between the two candidates, with Senator Cruz condemning the retweet as inappropriate and calling Trump a "sniveling

---

9 https://www.youtube.com/watch?v=-kjyltrKZSY.

coward" who tried to "smear" his wife—yet more evidence of carnivalesque name-calling spreading beyond Trump himself and the social media context. In the context of the Republican primary campaign that featured repeated attempts to slut-shame Melania Trump, it is not unusual that the wives of the primary candidates were included in the discussion, not to mention his female primary opponent Carly Fiorina whose face was supposedly not up to his standards. Melania Trump, a former model who arrived in the US on a talent visa, was constantly objectified and orientalized by her husband, mainstream media, comedians, and social media users (Wiedlack 2019). If during the Republican primaries the right-wing commentators focused on her modeling career and revealing photoshoots, once Trump became the Republican candidate, it was the left's turn to focus on her supposed sexualized transgressions and surgically enhanced looks (Weis 2023; Luthar 2023).

One of the most carnivalesque misogynistic moments of the 2015–2016 campaign was, however, the incident in the aftermath of the Republican primary debate moderated by then Fox host Megyn Kelly. In August 2015, Kelly asked Donald Trump about his past derogatory comments towards women: "You've called women you don't like 'fat pigs,' 'dogs,' 'slobs,' and 'disgusting animals.' … Does that sound to you like the temperament of a man we should elect as president?" After "correcting" Ms. Kelly, claiming that he had only referred to Rosie O'Donnell—which the audience laughed at—Trump replied:[10]

> I think the big problem this country has is being politically correct. I've been challenged by so many people, and I don't, frankly, have time for total political correctness. And to be honest with you, this country doesn't have time either. This country is in big trouble. We don't win anymore. We lose to China. We lose to Mexico … And you know what? I've been very nice to you, although I could probably maybe not be, based on the way you have treated me. But I wouldn't do that.

Trump's response has several hallmarks of carnival here. For starters, he bemoans the shackles of political correctness instead of confronting his own disrespectful attitude. He is also essentially threatening Kelly in this interaction: by not agreeing with Trump's rules of the game, Kelly might be downgraded to the level of those women he had previously insulted. Secondly, he legitimizes his misogynistic transgression by engaging a perceived sense of victimhood and veiled racist dog whistles by singling out non-white countries. Moreover, as Cuen and Evers (2016) demonstrate, in the 24-hour window after Trump refused to participate in a debate under her moderation, among the 80,000 tweets directed at Megyn Kelly's Twitter

---

10 https://www.youtube.com/watch?v=8f83CrDM0K4.

handle, the following words were included: bitch (n = 423), bimbo (n = 404), blonde (128), whore (n = 88), cheap (n = 66), ugly (n = 59), skank (n = 39), cunt (n = 34), slut (n = 27), and hooker (n = 13). This is entirely consistent with the kinds of abuse women are treated to during the carnival and outside of it.

Another carnivalesque outburst came after Trump was asked to comment on the altercation. Trump panned Kelly in his Don Lemon interview for CNN, saying her questions were "ridiculous" and "off-base." "You could see there was blood coming out of her eyes," "Blood coming out of her wherever."[11] He later clarified his comment on Twitter by stating that he was referring to Megyn Kelly's nose, but the phrase itself was widely interpreted as a derogatory and disrespectful re-mark towards women and it is of course a very carnivalesque one. Openly discus-sing bodily functions, blaming the woman for his own inadequacy, and transform-ing women into the abject are key features in this exchange. It is reminiscent of Klaus Theweleit's (1987) study of Freikorps soldiers in Germany before World War 2 who describe women as a red tide crashing against their bodies, becoming metonyms for what flows, unrooting them from the German soil in which they feel at home. This red flow-simultaneously communist, feminist, and menstrual-rever-berates in the Trump carnival's construction of the female abject. Even the conser-vative camp was openly critical of the remark and the clarification. Penny Young Nance, CEO and president of the conservative group Concerned Women for Amer-ica, told CNN that Trump's "tantrum was even more enlightening than his original remarks she [Ms. Kelly] questioned" (CNN Wire 2015)

As Bakhtin (2015) notes,

> The same carnival hell is an earth that absorbs and gives birth, it often turns into a cornuco-pia, the monster—death—turns out to be pregnant; various deformities—all these protruding bellies, huge noses, humps, etc.—turn out to be signs of pregnancy or reproductive force. (p. 45)

By discussing Kelly or Heidi Cruz in misogynistic terms, Trump is trying to make them into monsters that carnival ridicules and debases. The main issue here is the perceived loss of control over women.

For instance, 4chan users reveled in the "grab them by the pussy debate." For them it was an issue of dispensing with what some users called "gynocentrism," which they often attributed to antisemitic conspiracy myths, in which they associ-ate a women-centric world with "open borders. Regulating speech. Big government [...] Marxism, communism." In the end, some 4chan users expanded the metaphor

---

11 https://www.youtube.com/watch?v=UZdX6WHACnk.

to "grabbing civilization by the pussy" and restoring the influence to "MANkind."[12] This type of rhetoric is very reminiscent of Klaus Theweleit's (1987) analysis of the Nazi Freikorps argumentation: even the equation of women with Marxism and communism is eerily similar. The more typical 'American' contribution to the discourse is the association of the government with a 'nanny state.' According to Steven Ducat (2005), the 'nanny state' has been a particularly pervasive metaphor and object of fear in the right-wing political discourse as it is ultimately about the fear of emasculation and castration at the hands of women. The act of grabbing women's private parts is something that is obviously taboo—not only from a legal perspective, but also from a normative one. Yet, during carnival, this prohibition is somewhat lifted and much closer encounters are permitted. The hierarchy reversal almost necessitates the establishment of the domination of the women, who are seen as dangerous by their potential to emasculate the men. Thus, "grab civilization by the pussy" becomes a rallying cry of transgression, where 4chan users imagine taking control by transgressing the norms of civility and sanctity of other bodies.

While Trump sets a misogynist example, the swarm that adores him online takes carnivalesque misogyny even further. Male supremacism and misogyny have long been fundamental aspects of far-right culture (Ferber 1998; Daniels 2009; Carian et al. 2022). The specter of the woman, as we note with Theweleit above, is a metonymic figure in which woman stands simultaneously for the "red flood" of (Jewish) communism crashing against the sturdy men of Germany as well as the projection of male desire and potency. After the flood recedes, it leaves behind a sticky mire that taints everything, rendering modernity a kind of morass of degeneracy. This is, without any doubt, a white supremacist imaginary that is by no means temporally limited to interwar Germany. In the United States, fears about 'degeneracy' emerged from the earliest days of slavery and remain today in fears about the sexual propriety of white women, 'miscegenation,' and transgressions of their ideal heteronormative order. While the woman appears as a central figure of derision in carnivalesque populism, the stakes are high in that the perception of having control of women, their bodies, and particularly their reproductive capacity is paramount to the Trump carnival.

Coalfax, a website that lists and details white females and black males in relationships with one another, is perhaps one of the most extreme creations of the misogynist swarm that venerates Trump's derision of women. Using this platform as an extreme example, we will try to illustrate how the carnivalesque misogyny is

---

12 Based on the authors' analysis of their archive of collected 4chan posts of October and November 2016.

deeply connected to the racist and white supremacist aspects of the Trump carnival among his supporters, already referenced in the Twitter response to Megyn Kelly, above. Coalfax is probably the most despicable thing to come out of far-right digital cultures—at least, perhaps the most despicable thing to be seen on the public-facing web. Riffing on Carfax, which provides reports on vehicle data for customers interested in used cars, Coalfax was meant to be a repository where one could find a report on a white woman before dating her. In particular, it was a website that hosted a list of white women, whose pictures were stolen from Instagram for example, that were in sexual relationships with Black men. The "coal" half of the website's titular portmanteau comes from the white supremacist neologism, "coal burner," which refers to a white woman that dates Black men. It was a doxxing website, essentially organized in the so-called 'chanosphere' (see Baele and Brace 2021), where anons (members of the chanosphere) would collect information on women and post their photos and personal details from social media on the website. The women were categorized into four groups and organized with "tags." One of the tags was "toll paid," which refers to white women who dated Black men but now find themselves in a difficult situation, e. g., single motherhood, or in more extreme versions, victims of domestic violence and even murder. Tagging women on Coalfax with "toll paid" involves the direction of laughter and pleasure at the misfortune of these women. In this example, we see the intertwining of extreme racial and misogynistic imaginary in the transgression of even the most fundamental norms of decency.

In fact, Coalfax networks were too extreme even for 4chan and 8chan, and briefly found a home on the obscure 9chan. The website's domain changed a number of times; it was initially listed as coalfax.net before changing to coalfax.me and coalfax.ru (Baele and Brace 2021). Today it is completely unavailable, though vestiges and similar projects can be found on extremist platforms like Gab.ai and in obscure Telegram channels (see also Baele and Brace 2021). Coalfax represents many aspects of carnival coming together: the transgression of norms of decency by engaging in extreme defamation of women; the proliferation of multiple kinds of terms and insults to denigrate and dehumanize white women and the Black men with whom they were in relationships; and celebrating the misfortune of women whose relationships faltered or, in even more extreme cases, celebrating and reveling in the death of women at the hands of Black men because it fulfils the users' racist prophecies.

7.3 Anti-Clinton Discourse

Misogyny was an integral part of the 2016 election campaign (Boatright and Sperling 2019), which broadly reflects public opinion polls that indicated that American society is not entirely ready for a female president, even though between 2008 and 2017 that opposition has been cut in half, from 26% to 13% (Burden, Ono, and Yamada 2017; Streb et al. 2008). As Barbara Spackman notes, "in a fascist topography of gender and sex, stepping out into the public sphere 'masculinizes' and 'sterilizes' women" (Spackman 1996, p. 35). This line of argumentation was extremely visible in the anti-Hillary Clinton discourse that is genealogically linked to the Republican campaign against Bill Clinton's presidential campaign in the 1990s. The same ideas about 'ball-busting' first ladies—an integral carnivalesque fear—resurfaced again in their different iterations. Memes with Hillary Clinton being the shark from the movie Jaws that is supposed to devour the poor unsuspecting American created a parallel with one of the most common folkloric urban myths of the toothy vagina —vagina dentata (Otero 1996; Gaufman 2022), which is also a poignant carnival narrative (Noel 2010; Gilmore 2010).

As Ritchie argues, Hillary Clinton's image had already morphed with one of a monster or a cyborg during the 2008 presidential campaign (Ritchie 2013). During her competition with Barack Obama, multiple misogynistic jabs at her were taken, including memes that represented her as a Terminator. But even the liberal-leaning and Democratic forces often embraced the misogynistic rhetoric of the far right. If Trump supporters would don T-shirts emblazoned with the slogan "Trump that bitch," even SNL—in a broadcast on the eve of the election in October 2016, which racked up almost 30 million views—had Kate McKinnon as Hillary Clinton promising to be a "stone-cold B" in comparison to the F that a Trump presidency would be.[13] This goes to show that carnivalesque internalized misogyny was a staple during the presidential election campaign.

One of the most commonly cited examples of Trump's misogyny is his "nasty woman" remark (Smirnova 2018). On October 19, 2016, during the final presidential debate, the discussion turned to the topic of social security and each candidate's plans for it. Clinton criticized Trump's approach to the issue, suggesting that his plans would ultimately benefit the wealthy at the expense of working-class Americans. In response, Trump interrupted Clinton and referred to her as a "nasty woman."[14] In a very carnivalesque fashion, Trump sought to present Hillary Clinton as the 'old hag' of the carnivalesque procession. The remark garnered signifi-

---

13 https://www.youtube.com/watch?v=-kjyltrKZSY.
14 https://www.youtube.com/watch?v=Q2KOQfZ0Zd0.

cant attention and sparked widespread controversy and a backlash as sexist and disrespectful. Supporters of Clinton and women's rights advocates seized upon the incident as an example of the gender bias and derogatory language that women often face in politics and society. However, Clinton's supporters, especially many women, embraced the term 'nasty woman' as a symbol of empowerment, just like Trump supporters adopted Clinton's 'basket of deplorables' as a badge of honor and yet another sign of her disconnection from the 'real people'. It became a rallying cry and a badge of honor for many women who felt marginalized or dismissed by Trump's comments and his overall campaign rhetoric. Apart from "nasty woman" search queries, Google trends captures a very high interest in "nasty woman shirt" queries across almost all states.[15]

A fixation on the dangers of women's genitalia continued throughout Trump's presidency. In an attempt to reclaim the narrative from the right-wing misogynistic pundits, the late-night show comedian, Samantha Bee even instituted a special award in her *Full Frontal* show, called "Thundercunt" to honor journalists who have warned about Trump's danger to American society.[16] The first and last recipient of this award was CNN's journalist Jack Tapper who promised not to wear the T-Shirt that the *Full Frontal* team gave to him and not to mention the title of the award to his children. The term itself, according to Bee, emerged from Twitter. It was among the myriad instances of online abuse Bee herself had experienced over the years.

Bee's open critique of Trump did not stop at his presidency, but expanded additionally to his daughter Ivanka, who also assumed a role as "presidential advisor" in the Trump administration. The incident occurred on May 30, 2018, during a monologue about the Trump administration's immigration policies where Bee called out Donald Trump, former Attorney General Jeff Sessions, and former Secretary of Homeland Security Kirstjen Nielsen, as well as Ivanka. Amid the implementation of new racist immigration policies and the family separation scandal, Samantha Bee called Ivanka a "feckless cunt" because of Ms. Trump's failure to influence her dad's policies. Samantha Bee's comment sparked a significant backlash and controversy. Many viewers criticized her for using derogatory language and argued that it was inappropriate and disrespectful. *Buzzfeed News* complained that Ivanka deserved a "sharper critique" and not a "lazy insult" (Koul 2018); *The Guardian* argued that "cunt" remains the last word you cannot say on Amer-

---

15 https://trends.google.com/trends/explore?date=2016–01–01%202016–12–31&geo=US&q=nasty%20woman%20shirt&hl=en-US.
16 https://www.youtube.com/watch?v=SdOUspS-djo.

ican TV (Mahdawi 2018). Indeed, CBS news designated the term "a vulgar slur"[17] and ABC complained that the debate is over once comedy crosses the line.[18] Interestingly enough, two years prior to the incident, on another comedy show, Samantha Bee and Stephen Colbert performed a comedic bit on the different ways women can be allowed to reference their "bathing suit area."[19] In 2018, following the backlash, Samantha Bee issued an apology, expressing regret for her choice of words and acknowledging that they were offensive and inappropriate. Bee stated that she had intended to criticize Ivanka Trump's actions and not to attack her personally. The incident fueled discussions about the boundaries of acceptable language in political discourse and the role of civility in public debate: it seemed that transgression was only legitimate and allowed in the case of male participants of the carnival.

Of course, it is not only men who engage in (online) misogyny. Internalized misogyny was an important factor in shaping Trump's presidential campaign and his presidency, where a number of female pundits and politicians engaged in anti-Clinton rhetoric from a gendered angle (Strolovitch, Wong, and Proctor 2017; Kunemund 2019). It is widely considered that gender played an important role in the 2016 election campaign. Moreover, the gender issue did not seem to make any changes to Trump followers online (Wang et al. 2016): they stuck with him no matter what.

The misogyny did not stop with Trump's election. During his presidency he invariably attacked not only Hillary Clinton, but also new members of Congress, especially women of color, and in particular, the so-called "Squad," consisting of four women elected in the 2018 United States House of Representatives elections: Alexandria Ocasio-Cortez of New York, Ilhan Omar of Minnesota, Ayanna Pressley of Massachusetts, and Rashida Tlaib of Michigan. All four have been the target of vicious attacks by Trump himself and his online supporters who have engaged in disgusting behavior on their message boards. Alexandria Ocasio-Cortez, also known as AOC, who is often perceived as a populist herself (Cooper and Avery 2021), has been an especial target of numerous death threats, rape threats, and hate speech. Trump, for instance, has said that the four congresswomen should "go back and help fix the totally broken and crime-infested places from which they came" (Pengelly 2019). 4chan users alternated between lusting after AOC and re-

---

17 https://www.youtube.com/watch?v=d5tYcliU3jA&pp=ygUaZmVja2lc3MgY3VudCBzYW1hbnRoRoYS-BiZWU%3D.

18 https://www.youtube.com/watch?v=N5hQbAdfuGQ&pp=ygUaZmVja2lc3MgY3VudCBzYW1hbn-RoYSBiZWU%3D.

19 https://www.youtube.com/watch?v=Q8MbSwCd78M.

telling violent fantasies about "putting her in her place."[20] Just as in the 16th century France, the carnivalesque "rites of violence" (Zemon Davis 1971) were supposed to discipline supposedly domineering women, the online mob tried to find an "iron muzzle" to silence and punish the women they don't like.

Misogyny is an integral part of the carnival. While it is supposedly anti-authority and intended to enable the inversion of power, women and femininity altogether tended to stay put in the same heteronormative niche. The only temporary dispensation accorded was permitted promiscuity, but again, it carried stigma only for women, not for men, just like outside of carnival as well. The central role in the carnival is played by the fool, a male fool, who can be funny and allow himself to be ridiculed, especially if he is in on the joke, just like Trump was featured in all those SNL skits. For women, this role is much more precarious. As we explain below, 'funny women' have traditionally been restricted to several (visual) stereotypes, often dictated by carnival culture (Porter 1998). A fat, cheerful man can have a political career outside of carnival. A woman of the same stature not so much, at least, not yet.

---

20 Based on the authors' analysis of their archive of collected 4chan posts of October and November 2016.

Chapter 8: Sex and Materiality

Given that carnival is an antithesis of normal, highly religious Renaissance life, the former is also fascinated with the material aspects of existence. Hence, people are obsessed with body parts, bodily functions, sex, and material objects during carnival. As such, the body itself was supposed to be highlighted and represented in a very grotesque way. As Bakhtin himself noted (Bakhtin 2015):

> the grotesque body is not delimited from the rest of the world, it is not closed, it is not complete, it is not ready, it outgrows itself, goes beyond its own limits. The accents lie on those parts of the body where it is either open to the outside world, that is, where the world enters the body or sticks out of it, or it sticks out into the world itself, that is, on holes, on bulges, on all sorts of branches and processes: open mouth, reproductive organ, breasts, phallus, fat belly, nose. The body reveals its essence as a growing and transcending principle only in such acts as copulation, pregnancy, childbirth, agony, eating, drinking, defecation. [...] This is always a fraught and birthing body, or at least a body that is ready for conception and fertilization—with an emphasized phallus or reproductive organ. (pp. 17–18)

In the quote above, Bakhtin emphasizes the transgressive nature of the body itself. By displaying the body, its orifices, and appendages, which are otherwise cloaked with clothing, carnival seeks to liberate not only the flesh but also the different bodily functions that the bounds of civilization are supposed to hide. Comedy shows constantly alluded to Trump's mouth as resembling a butthole (Jones 2017; Gilbert 2019) thus building a metonym such that whatever emerges from it is feces. There is even a whole philosophical theory about Donald Trump being an asshole (Meyer 2016; James 2016; Wahl-Jorgensen 2019), which again shows that even his critics engaged in the mode of carnivalesque abjection where the ridiculed person is supposed to be degraded to the extreme, physical bottom.

During the campaign though, as noted in the chapter on misogyny, it was women who were the targets of the carnivalesque abuse. No wonder that one of the most common ways of illustrating carnivalesque transgression is a fat female body (Braziel and LeBesco 2001; Arthurs 1999), a trope extremely common in American popular culture that is almost by default supposed to be raunchy, obscene, and "low class" (Warner and Savigny 2015): a quintessential carnivalesque. During the presidential election campaign, one of the main targets of Trump's ire was comedian Rosie O'Donnell, whom he called a "fat pig."[21] If a fat female body is supposed to be funny in this male gaze, and to signify the grotesque, then certain types of female bodies are meant to be the object of another, lustful gaze.

---

21 https://www.youtube.com/watch?v=ASd4-Vo7RAU.

The pre-Christian origins of carnival were related to fertility rituals and connected to practices of phallic worship (Ahye 2000; Harris 2003; Cowan 1994). Moreover, the whole notion of carnival celebrates flesh and the sexuality associated with it, even though outside of the carnivalesque period, this celebration is not necessarily acceptable (Perkins 2011). This dichotomy is very visible in postcolonial readings of carnivalesque traditions, especially in the Caribbean, where celebration of the body was a transgression against the colonizer's ideology and rule (Cowan 1994; Outar 2017), not to mention an opportunity to perform a transgressive sexuality (Persadie 2021; Donnell 2014). Performing transgressive sexuality in the colonized context is an act of resistance, but what happens when the sexuality that is performed is very much in line with the dominant views? The transgression then moves to the area of displaced abjection, where non-conforming bodies are subjected to ridicule and violence. While the grotesque is a vital part of the ridicule and embodied experience, it is the metaphorical and sometimes literal bottom that should be the focus in carnival:

> In the Middle Ages, a cheerful parodic grammar was very common [...]. The essence of this merry grammar boils down to the main way to rethink all grammatical categories—cases, forms of verbs and etc.—in the material and bodily plane, mainly erotic one. But not only parodies in the narrow sense, but also all other forms of grotesque realism reduce, land, make things corporeal. This is the main feature of grotesque realism, distinguishing it from all forms of high art and literature of the Middle Ages. Folk laughter, which organizes all forms of grotesque realism, has always been associated with the material bodily bottom. Laughter lowers the register and materializes. (Bakhtin 2005, p. 14)

As Ravenscroft and Gilchrist (2009) argue, there is a "hegemonic regulatory function" performed by the licensing of practices in gay pride parades. By restricting open celebration and the spectacle of queer bodies to a certain period of time, the gay pride parade does not necessarily normalize or mainstream the queer experience for the rest of the population. Of course, these celebrations are important to queer communities; but like the carnival, they do not inherently normalize queerness. In fact, pride parades have been used by autocrats to legitimize abhorrent anti-liberal policies and regimes. For instance, Russian Patriarch Kirill even claimed that the Russia's 2022 invasion of Ukraine was launched to prevent a gay pride parade in Donetsk (Moscow Times 2022).

8.1 Sex Sells

Let us not blame all the sex-centered discourse on Trump. As Matthew Baum has long argued, sex scandals have been the face of so-called soft news that helps sell even boring foreign policy to the inattentive public (Baum 2002). One of the authors of this book, who was a teenager during the 1990s (it does not matter who), still remembers the avalanche of media reporting on what was back in the day called "The Monica Lewinsky scandal." Of course, this was a very misogynistic way of reporting on the case of power abuse and infidelity perpetrated by one of the most powerful men in the world—former US President Bill Clinton. The media obsession with the minute details of the case led to many awkward sex-education-related conversations in one of the households that produced this book. Needless to say, the post-Soviet school system was not prepared to handle the discussions about different types of liquids, euphemisms for intercourse, and body shapes that the mass media around the world were eager to report. While there were no social media at the time, Monica Lewinsky became one of the most brutally shamed people in the world through the Internet (Dahl 2016) and by late-night comedians (Farnsworth and Lichter 2019), with the phrase "oral sex" appearing 162 times in *The New York Times* alone in 1998. While it is impossible to assess the exact impact the Bill Clinton sex scandal and subsequent impeachment trial had on American politics (Miller 1999), it has certainly influenced the way media normalized the discussion of sex acts on prime-time TV and in newspapers. On Amazon, it is still possible to buy "Hillary sucks but not like Monica" T-shirts, which are sold as a "funny election T-shirt." Customers who bought it complained that the product smelled bad. We wonder why.

As carnival is laser focused on copulation, it is no wonder that male organs are supposed to be on discursive display. The world of carnivalesque phallic worship was especially visible due to the remarks made by another Republican presidential candidate—Marco Rubio. In early 2016, Rubio, seeking to criticize Trump, stated, "And you know what they say about guys with small hands ... You can't trust them" (Jaffe 2016). The comment was seen as an attempt to mock Trump's physical appearance and, by extension, his manhood, indirectly questioning Trump's suitability for the presidency. It harked back to an old insult that had occasionally been directed at Trump over the years, suggesting that small hands were a sign of inadequacy or weakness. During a subsequent debate Trump felt compelled to defend the size of his hands, asserting that they were actually normal-sized and dismissing the notion that hand size correlated with any other aspect of a person's attributes. The controversy surrounding Trump's hand size gained significant media attention and became a topic of discussion during the campaign and was extolled ad nauseam by both mainstream news media and comedy shows with headlines such as "Trump defends size of his manhood, 'little hands'" by ABC

News[22] and "Trump defends his hands—again" by CNN,[23] with even supposedly sophisticated outlets like *The New Yorker* mocking Trump's hands.

In the carnivalesque world of phallic worship, this incident provides a great illustration of how the election campaign had functioned on the level of the corporeal and 'low culture.' It is also indicative that Trump was not the one who initiated the discussion: in multidirectional discourse with multiple voices it is inevitable that someone else engages in the discussion about male appendages. Previously, these kinds of discussions in American politics were only implied and never discussed so openly (Appadurai 2021; Berger 2016), unless projected onto gun worship (Blanchfield 2018; Cohn 1987).

Another transgressive body manifestation was illustrated by the infamous *Access Hollywood* Tape that surfaced during the 2016 elections campaign. The scandal revolved around a leaked video that captured a conversation between Trump and Billy Bush, a television host, during their appearance on the entertainment news program, *Access Hollywood*, in 2005. The video, which was released by *The Washington Post* on October 7, 2016, featured a private conversation between Trump and Bush, where Trump made lewd and sexually explicit remarks about women. In the video, Trump boasted about using his celebrity status to engage in non-consensual sexual advances towards women, including comments about groping women without their consent. The remarks were widely condemned for promoting and normalizing sexual assault.

The revelation of the *Access Hollywood* Tape caused significant political turmoil during the presidential campaign. Trump faced immense backlash both within his own party and from the general public. Many prominent Republican leaders condemned his remarks, with some withdrawing their support or calling for him to step aside as the nominee. The scandal dominated headlines and further fueled the already contentious nature of the 2016 election. Even saying the word "pussy" on air was a transgressive challenge for a number of American pundits (Cameron 2020), where the anchors struggled and danced around the term that Trump had used. Even *The Daily Show* with Trevor Noah put asterisks in its description of what it called a "P***ygate Scandal."[24] Large-scale protests against Trump's election in November 2016 created a whole industry of knitting and selling pink "pussy hats" (Gökarıksel and Smith 2017) that continued the handcrafted tradition of protest (Mandell 2019). Carnival is a marketplace too, after all.

---

22 https://www.youtube.com/watch?v=Ve6I92hEozo&pp=ygUSdHJ1bXAgaGFuZHMgY29tZWR5.
23 https://www.cnn.com/2016/03/21/politics/donald-trump-defends-hand-size/index.html.
24 https://www.youtube.com/watch?v=LiPjWUn-PUo.

Carnival's emphasis on material rather than spiritual life was particularly prominent in the Trump campaign. It was especially true for the focus on body parts. For what was probably a first, the size of a presidential candidate's penis actually came up during an American election debate (Mathis-Lilley 2016). One can argue that the physical features of presidential candidates have become increasingly important with the advent of TV and the visualization of politics (Bleiker 2016; Williams 2003; Hansen 2011), but none of the previous presidential campaigns were so extensively covered by news media and especially social media. Hardly any comedic segment on CBS, NBC, HBO, or Comedy Central failed to mention the size of Trump's allegedly small hands (Hopper 2016), his hair, or the color of his skin (e. g., "orange Hitler"), which is ridiculous in a political debate, yet normal in a carnival setting. Trump himself seems to be obsessed with body parts and close physical contact, as, for instance, his association with WWE and even active participation in matches shows. At the same time, wrestling has itself been identified as having carnival roots (Campbell 1996; Sehmby 2002), so the extent to which Donald Trump is a representative of carnival culture is itself grotesque.

Trump's philandering (Foran 2016) was particularly galling in respect of the traditional importance of the president of the United States' moral character, and showed that the 2016 election campaign genuinely signified a complete reversal of politics as usual. The (perhaps not so) surprisingly high voter support for Trump among evangelical and born-again Christian voters (Martínez and Smith 2016) can be primarily explained by carnival culture. Given that carnival is a temporary phenomenon and that it represents another life that one can live until repenting one's sins, many Trump voters stressed that they did not take Trump literally and admitted that his campaign was a way of winning office and did not reflect his true attitudes (Berman 2016).

Another side of this obsession with the body was related to the media and regular people's tendencies to focus on the body of the former First Lady Melania Trump, as well as Trump's opponent Hillary Clinton. In the latter case, Trump focused, in classic carnivalesque fashion, on ridiculing the supposedly infirm and weak body of his opponent, mocking her by exclaiming that he thought that she "needed a nap."[25] The grass roots inversion of that trope was the infamous body double conspiracy myth that was popular on social media in the US and beyond (Linvill and Warren 2020; Gaufman 2023). According to the purveyors of this discredited theory, Hillary Clinton died of pneumonia and was replaced by a body double during the election campaign. The body double conspiracy is a carnivalesque phenomenon as it was very common for two actors to share one mask

---

25 https://www.youtube.com/watch?v=YvVOBJShGgg.

(Roach 1995) or try to deceive the audience by having one actor wearing a mask or by means of one person wearing several masks.

As we mention above, focus on the body is vital in carnivalesque culture. Laughing about the body is integral and of course, laughing over disfigured or disabled bodies has been a staple of the carnival for centuries. In Trump's case, the target was Serge Kovaleski. Serge Kovaleski is a Pulitzer Prize-winning journalist who had previously worked for *The Washington Post* and currently works for *The New York Times.* He has a congenital joint condition, arthrogryposis, which affects the movement of his arms. During the rally, Trump criticized Kovaleski for an article he had written in 2001, which claimed Trump supported the false assertion that thousands of Muslims in New Jersey celebrated the 9/11 attacks. As Trump spoke, he said, "poor guy, you got to see this guy" and flailed his arms and imitated Kovaleski's physical disability,[26] seemingly mocking his mannerisms. The incident received widespread criticism from various quarters, including journalists, disability advocacy groups, and political opponents, although the crowd at the rally seemed to laugh at Trump's 'impersonation.' Many viewed Trump's actions as offensive and disrespectful, particularly toward people with disabilities. Trump, however, denied that he was mocking Kovaleski's disability and insisted that he did not know what the journalist looked like, which was, of course, a lie. At the same time, Fox News created a compilation of Trump clips, most of them from after the Kovaleski incident, where he appeared to mock other people like Ted Cruz, bank regulators, and US generals with somewhat similar 'physical comedy.' For the people in the comments section, that was evidence enough that the mocking was ok.[27]

8.2 Violent Fantasies

While the incel movement obviously predates the Trump campaign, in many ways this ideology was emboldened by Trump, in part as a manifestation of carnival. The term 'incel' is a portmanteau of "involuntary celibate." It refers to an online subculture consisting of predominantly heterosexual men who claim to be unable to find sexual or romantic relationships despite their desires and efforts. Incels often congregate in online forums and communities where they discuss their experiences, frustrations, and beliefs. Some incel communities have gained notoriety for promoting misogynistic, violent, and hateful ideologies. Certain individuals within these communities express resentment and hostility towards women, blam-

---

26 https://www.youtube.com/watch?v=hFOy8-03qdg&t=19s.
27 https://www.youtube.com/watch?v=CsaB3ynIZH4.

ing them for their perceived lack of romantic or sexual success. Such views can manifest as misogyny, objectification, and even advocacy for violence against women. In other words, as Kelly and Aunsprach (2020) point out, incel discourse is "a white militant extension of compulsory sexuality that transforms alternative intimacies into violent masculinist fantasies of invulnerability and the sexual will-to-power" (p. 149). Essentially, by mainstreaming incel discourse, American media have changed the way in which conversations about sex are carried out (Bogetic 2023). Incels also use humor, which gives them (im)plausible deniability (Gothard 2021), but at their core they promote a reactionary and in many ways transgressive rhetoric that seeks to subjugate women and minorities.

An example of the 'new way' in which conversations about sex were carried out is Trump's speech at the 2017 Boy Scout Jamboree (Regan 2017). In front of a crowd of teenagers, Trump waxed poetic about the glory days of one of his friends (?):

> And he sold his company, for a tremendous amount of money, at the time especially. This is a long time ago. Sold his company for a tremendous amount of money. And he went out and bought a big yacht, and he had a very interesting life. I won't go any more than that, because you're Boy Scouts so I'm not going to tell you what he did.

Judging by the enthusiastic reception given to the speech, the Boy Scouts knew full well what Trump was not talking about. Apart from Jamboree capturing the atmosphere of one of Trump's own rallies, where adoring crowds applaud and chant to Trump's meandering monologues, the teenage boys were also drawn into the spectacle of Trump's desirability by association with the supposedly decadent uber rich world of manly men. Do boys want to grow up like him? We hope not.

Trump's physical characteristics did not necessarily lend to the creation of a profoundly virile image. That is why many supporters sought to amplify his masculinity through traditional visual means by depicting him in a more conventionally homoerotic and muscular way: numerous images of Trump with exaggerated pectoral muscles and biceps, featuring weapons, large cars, and other supposed attributes of manhood, became very common on social media, often re-tweeted by Trump himself or sold at his rallies by his supporters. Thus, even Trump himself was no longer embodied through his own physique but rather through the virile fantasy of what (probably he himself and) his supporters aspire to. This was a grotesque and unrealistic representation of virility that was supposed to reverse the hierarchy of what many of his supporters conceived of as a women-centric world. Trump's photoshopped muscled body was often featured on T-shirts that are still sold on Amazon and are still sold at his rallies. The image of Trump as a muscular bodybuilder in the vein of Arnold Schwarzenegger or Silvester Stallone serves as an avatar or even as a carnivalesque costume for his supporters to embrace. The grotesque steroid-enhanced body, the overly emphasized muscles, the fleshiness that is supposed to convey extreme masculinity and desirability. At some point, Trump himself reposted a meme of his head photoshopped onto Silvester Stallone's character, Rocky Balboa, the boxer from the eponymous movie. At the time, *The Guardian* posited that "no one knows what to make of it," but we do know what to make of it (Noor 2019). By hiding behind yet another mask of a muscular and hypothetically desirable man, he means to inherit those qualities himself and his base are supposed to pretend that this is why they vote for him.

The same applies to the images of Trump as a superhero. As Julian Schmid writes, comic books and specifically the superhero genre have a disproportionate effect on the way American politics is conceptualized (Schmid 2020). Moreover, the politics of superheroes, the vigilante ethos, and other hallmarks of the genre resonate with post-9/11 US foreign policy (Dittmer 2011, 2016). So it is no wonder that the genre and the cultural artifacts associated with it became a part and parcel of Trump's own rhetoric and his support. While many people dress as superheroes for Halloween, Trump and his base often dressed him up as such online, with Trump at some point even suggesting that he is as inevitable as Thanos, a super-villain appearing in American comic books published by Marvel Comics (Boje 2020; Knopf 2021). In a sense, Trump was right: he was inevitable. Whether we want it or not, the press will platform him as a former president. At the same time, it was remarkable that Stephen Colbert refused to say the former president's name on his show, correctly identifying Trump's brand as one of his strengths and instituting a type of cordon sanitaire, at least on this level of media engagement (De Jonge and Gaufman 2022).

8.3 The Stormy Daniels Affair

In 2011, it was reported that Donald Trump had had an affair with Stormy Daniels, an adult film star. According to Ms. Daniels, the affair lasted for several months. Trump, who was married to his current wife Melania Trump at the time, has denied the affair. However, as the 2016 presidential election neared, it was alleged that in October 2016 an agreement was made between Trump's personal lawyer, Michael Cohen, and Stormy Daniels in order to conceal the affair. The agreement involved a $130,000 payment to Daniels as part of a nondisclosure agreement (NDA) to keep the affair confidential. In January 2018, *The Wall Street Journal* published a report revealing the existence of the alleged hush money payment. This disclosure led to widespread media coverage and public attention surrounding the affair and the arrest of Michael Cohen, who pled guilty to federal campaign finance regulations and tax evasion in relation to the scandal. Following the public revelation,

Stormy Daniels filed a lawsuit seeking to invalidate the NDA, claiming that it was void because Trump did not sign it. She also argued that the agreement violated campaign finance laws. Trump and his legal team sought to enforce the NDA. Amid the controversy, other women came forward with allegations of past affairs with Trump or of being subjected to inappropriate behavior by him. Notable among them was Karen McDougal, a former Playboy model who claimed to have had a relationship with Trump around the same time as the alleged affair with Ms. Daniels. In 2018, Trump's legal team and Stormy Daniels reached a settlement, resulting in the dismissal of the lawsuit. As part of the agreement, Ms. Daniels was released from the NDA, allowing her to speak publicly about the alleged affair. And speak she did.

Apart from the numerous interviews in mainstream media, including the very reputable "60 Minutes," Stormy Daniels appeared on several late-night shows: for instance, she was featured in an SNL skit—"Michael Cohen Wiretap Cold Open"[28] —where she played herself, made jokes about her line of work and "not being known for her acting," asked Trump to resign, and made a double entendre about climate change. On Jimmy Kimmel, she gave an 11-minute interview in which she "talk[ed] about the press release that just came out saying that the affair with Donald Trump never happened, the aftermath of the Trump sex scandal, whether or not she has a non-disclosure agreement, Trump bringing the three women who accused Bill Clinton of inappropriate sexual behavior to a debate with Hillary, the In Touch article, the size of Trump's junk, and plays a round of 'Never Have I Ever.'"[29] Even the description on YouTube featured the penis discussion, not to mention the fact that after Ms. Daniels revelation, a mushroom emoji has also become yet another way to mock Trump and discuss his supposed physical inadequacy. The numerous innuendos and puns that *The Late Show* with Stephen Colbert used in Colbert's monologue descriptions had some kind of reference to sex: "Trump's less than magic mushroom," "Porn Star Wars," "the fellate show," "spank of America" are only some of the banners that were used to discuss the actual case of campaign finance violation, which was reduced to the discussion of sex and body parts.

One of the more initially bewildering shows of support for Trump's campaigns and presidency came from the white evangelical electorate. Evangelical leaders David Brody, Jerry Falwell Jr., Franklin Graham, and Robert Jeffress defended Trump during the scandal because he was supposedly an "imperfect vessel" sent to protect evangelical values (Smith and Connable 2021). However, evangelical

---

28 https://www.youtube.com/watch?v=K1K8s-tQGqY.
29 https://www.youtube.com/watch?v=Ntl5Da1vblI.

Christian support for Trump is not at all surprising if we look at his candidacy through the carnivalesque lens. The act of essentially legitimizing sexual transgression and misogyny fits well with the transitive nature of the carnival that is supposed to uphold the existing social order. In other words, Trump did deliver on some of his promises to the evangelical electorate, including the ultra-conservative Supreme Court. Carnival does allow sexual transgression as long as once it is over the transgressor can pray for forgiveness and return to the fold. Trump did not even have to pray for forgiveness for his actions.

Another mode of sexual transgression that the media latched onto was the emphasis on Trump fantasizing about having sex with his daughter Ivanka. SNL also joked about mistaking his current wife Melania for a "Bangable daughter" in a cold open in October 2015 that amassed 15 million views.[30] And in their cold open about the last presidential debate on October 23, 2016, Kate McKinnon, impersonating Hillary Clinton, produced a bingo card of what Trump was supposed to have said, featuring a square with "If she wasn't my daughter."[31] Incest is one of society's most harsh taboos, so it was not surprising that Trump's comments on the sexual attractiveness of his daughter were taken literally and blown out of proportion. After all, as a long-time owner of the Miss Universe pageant, Trump probably considered himself an expert on women's physical attractiveness and wanted to increase his status by associating with beautiful women and claiming their beauty as his.

Sex and materiality are obviously part of life. While consumerism is often celebrated discussing the latest sexual exploits and kinks is supposedly "locker room talk"—Trump's justification for the *Access Hollywood* Tape. Even though it seems that there is much less stigma associated with queerness and non-traditional relationships in popular culture, there is also a massive backlash towards this visibility among the reactionary and very mobilized electorate. There is a reason that Ron DeSantis is trying to capitalize on Trump's supposed leniency towards the queer community. There is also a reason why the ironic "Thanks, Obama!" has morphed into the "Fuck Joe Biden!" chant at Republican rallies. It's not about a sex-positive environment, it's about establishing dominance via the only method the far right can imagine.

---

30 https://www.youtube.com/watch?v=Ft5XUalItuY.
31 https://www.youtube.com/watch?v=-kjyltrKZSY.

Chapter 9: Conclusion

This project started in 2016 after a sleepless night watching the election result forecasting tool of the *New York Times*, the 'needle', slowly lean towards the red side on November 8. Incredulity over Trump's victory quickly translated into "Not My President's Day" marches across the United States in February 2017. Four years of Trump's presidency followed—something that even SNL comedians did not predict. Despite the funny sketches, there was nothing to laugh about outside of the studio. On the other hand, once Trump lost the elections in 2020, his supporters engaged in the ultimate carnivalesque act of reclaiming the power that they thought was taken away from them. By claiming that the elections were rigged, even ahead of his own 2016 win, Trump eroded his public's trust in this democratic institution. Hence, the storming of the Capitol in January 2021: while Trump may have thought that he could hold on to power by instigating the insurrection, material from the January 6 Commission shows a significant number of people believed they had the right to transgress: to break down doors, windows, defecate in public, steal, declare that 6 million dead Jews were not enough, and wear horned fur hats in the chambers. And yet, many analysts consider a 2024 Trump win a distinct possibility.

Bakhtin's carnival is "the apotheosis of unfinalizability" (Morson and Emerson 1990). What this means is that whatever happens during the carnival will not continue beyond it: everyone knows that carnival is limited. So whatever reversal of hierarchy or merriment you enjoy during it will be over sooner or later, when Lent takes over. This unfinalizability was a hallmark of the Trump campaign: only a handful of people believed in the Trump win during the first election campaign; many thought the campaign was the ultimate goal in itself, for branding or other reasons. So what happens, when Lent does not follow the carnival? What are you supposed to do when the carnival fool who grabs women by the pussy actually becomes the town's mayor, or, in this case, the head of one of the most powerful states in the world? This is when all the supposed merriment of carnival starts to sour. Once the carnival fool who wants to burn the witches is in power, who will be able to stop them? There is ample evidence that once populists come to power, they continue the demonization practices on which they campaigned (Pirro and Taggart 2023). As a political strategy, carnival is ambivalent: it can liberate the marginalized, but as we have seen, it can unleash reactionary tendencies that exacerbate oppression rather than overturn the status quo. It will not lead to the political change it professes, because ultimately, it will keep things the way they are and make things worse for those who were never in power.

Trump's carnival has fundamentally altered American politics. On the right, the carnival has never stopped. The transgression of the basic norms of democracy remains a feature of its politics. This is most evident in the fact that each time Donald Trump has been charged with crimes that include election fraud—despite him having sworn to uphold the Constitution—Republicans *increase* their support for him. In Florida, Ron DeSantis has pushed forward an obscene revision of the historiography of slavery, with grade school class lessons expected to refer to the useful 'skills' that slaves had learned. Along with Texas Governor Greg Abbot, DeSantis and their Republican supporters take joy in defrauding migrants and asylum seekers, sending them to Martha's Vineyard and the Naval Observatory in DC in order to "own the libs." Having once reached their destination, the people were stranded, unhoused, without food, and often many miles away from the courts where they had to appear in order to have their asylum application considered. The inhumanity of treating the people this way, despite their legal right to claim asylum, is a show that speaks only to the cruelty and inhumanity that Trump's carnival has normalized. This callous and unconscionable endeavor—sending some of the most vulnerable people in the world to cities across the US with no regard to their obligation to appear in courts in entirely different parts of the country just to make a political point—is a despicable transgression of even the most basic norms of human dignity. The cruelty is also the point in the carnival culture as well. Sometimes it's about physical abuse, often about ridicule. By scapegoating marginalized groups, connoting them as revolting and incapable of assimilation, it is possible to normalize the engagment in racist rhetoric as carnivalesque freedom.

The ferocity with which the GOP's base support Trump demonstrates the enduring power of the carnival. Trump can violate the Constitution, yet the throngs of carnival-goers at his ralies and his supporters in opinion polls in 2023 suggest that these violations even enhance Trump's standing in his base. The more cruelty is expressed, the more the norms of decency, humanity, and dignity are violated, the more the righteousness of Trump's politics are affirmed. Today, as we approach the Republican primary, it is clear that Trump has deeply altered right-wing politics in the US. This is particularly evident when we look at what is likely to be the ephemeral arc of Vivek Ramaswamy, the biotech huckster running in the Republican primary, who frequently castigates the 'victim culture' of the left, yet—just like other far-right politicians—constantly synthesizes the falsehood that 'woke' culture, 'political correctness,' and 'diversity' are marginalizing everyday (read: 'white') Americans. This victim culture is endemic to the right, and is central to the transgressions of the Trump carnival. Ramaswamy's proposals—such as laying off vast swathes of the federal government or changing the voting age—are so ludicrous they could only be conceived in the suspension of truth that sustains the

Trump carnival. What is frightening is that it seems the pundits and producers in the broadcast industry have learned almost nothing from 2016; Ramaswamy's bellicosity and polemic certainly make for great TV (just like Trump), but the constant invitations he receives only give him more opportunity to pander to the excesses of the carnivalesque square that Trump's campaign established.

Carnival reinforces existing societal hierarchy and safeguards the prevailing social order. It is no inherently revolutionary force for the liberation of anything other than the will for domination and power amongst those forlorn to lose their sanctioned superiority in the advance of democracy. More ominously, it provides discursive legitimization for violence against marginalized groups. We are not positivists at all in our analysis, but even we can recognize a spike of violence towards marginalized communities in the US. Southern Poverty Law Center 2016 statistics show an increase in anti-immigrant and anti-Black, anti-LGBTQ, antisemitic and anti-Muslim crimes. Trump's racist rhetoric correlates with this uptick in racist crimes. Trump calls Covid "the China virus" and an anti-Asian hate crime wave engulfs the country. Words matter, especially those that strip the humanity from people already marginalized by the existing social structures. A laughing culture cannot be an excuse for racism; it has been so for too long. When you laugh at blackface 'Jim Crow' and treat him as an object of pleasurable consumption, it suddenly seems normal to deny him rights and humanity. It's just a joke, chill! It is political correctness that is the real oppressor![32]

One of the main differences between Trump's carnival and the original carnival is the extent of the elite's involvement in the carnival. After all, in the latter, it is their decision to allow it to happen. They also serve as a punchline for jokes. But the Trump carnival was different. Not only because in many ways he assumed the central role to be played in the carnival—the trickster—but also because by employing carnivalesque techniques, he made himself less vulnerable to the carnivalesque critiques of his opponents. He was right when he said that if he shoots somebody in the middle of Fifth Avenue, nothing will happen. Transgression becomes cool, a mark of accomplishment, a feature of "winning" and "owning the libs" who are stupid enough to follow all those rules. The fact that Trump's indictments haven't affected his approval rating (if anything, they have had a positive effect) shows that transgression perpetrated by those in power is completely legitimized. We could also include a *Family Guy* skin color matrix to show that Trump being

---

[32] Just in case someone takes these two last sentences out of context, we are being sarcastic! For the record, we do not think that political correctness is the real oppressor. And while you are reading this footnote, slavery was bad too, despite current Republican attempts to rephrase it as "slaves learning useful skills."

white plays a critical role, but if you reached this conclusion, you already know that from the rest of the book.

While this book focused on the Trump election campaign and presidency, the carnivalesque framework can also help us de-provincialize Trump (Rosa and Bonilla 2017): the ideology of transgression, white supremacy, colonial and racial legacies are often part of other carnivalesque candidates' bids for power. Yet, it is important to note that currently, there is another presidential candidate in the US that embraces many of Trump's policies without the trickster flair and other carnivalesque practices—Ron DeSantis. However, without the laughing culture and sex, his policies can be categorized as simply fascist (Giroux 2022). Whether the other GOP candidates will be the Lent that ends the Trump carnival remains to be seen, though it seems the square remains abuzz. After all they are not far from each other policy-wise. The carnival is not over, the rules are broken and it is up to Americans themselves to fix them.

Bibliography

Abdelkader, Engy. 2016. *When Islamophobia Turns Violent: The 2016 US Presidential Elections*. The Bridge Initiative, Georgetown University.

Abrajano, Marisa, and Zoltan L Hajnal. 2015. "White backlash." In *White Backlash*. Princeton University Press.

Ahye, Geraldine Molly. 2000. *Parade and Dance of Masqueraders in Trinidad and Tobago Carnivals: Epiphany of Dionysos/Bacchus:* New York University.

Aiolfi, Théo. 2022. "Populism as a transgressive style." *Global Studies Quarterly* 2 (1):ksac006.

Al-Ghazzi, Omar. 2021. "We will be great again: Historical victimhood in populist discourse." *European Journal of Cultural Studies* 24 (1):45 – 59.

Alcoff, Linda. 1996. "Dangerous pleasures: Foucault and the politics of pedophilia." In *Feminist Interpretations of Michel Foucault*, 99 – 136. Pennsylvania State University Press.

Anderson, Ben, and Anna Secor. 2022. "Propositions on right-wing populism: Available, excessive, optimistic." *Political Geography* 96:102608.

Anderson, Chris. 2008. "The end of theory: The data deluge makes the scientific method obsolete." *Wired*, June 23. https://www.wired.com/2008/06/pb-theory/.

Andrews, Edna. 1996. "Cultural sensitivity and political correctness: The linguistic problem of naming." *American Speech* 71 (4):389 – 404.

Appadurai, Arjun. 2021. *Trump and the Death of the Image*. Wiley Online Library.

Arbour, Brian. 2018. "This Is Trump Country: Donald Trump's base and partisan change in unhyphenated America." In *American Political Parties Under Pressure: Strategic Adaptations for a Changing Electorate*, 15 – 42. Palgrave Macmillan.

Archive of Political Emails. 2023. Donald Trump. https://politicalemails.org/organizations/415.

Arthurs, Jane. 1999. "Revolting women: the body in comic performance." In *Women's Bodies: Discipline and Transgression*, 137 – 164. Cassell.

Austin, Algernon. 2015. *America Is not Post-racial: Xenophobia, Islamophobia, Racism, and the 44th President:* ABC-CLIO.

Awan, Imran. 2014. "Islamophobia and Twitter: A typology of online hate against Muslims on social media." *Policy & Internet* 6 (2):133 – 150. https://doi.org/10.1002/1944-2866.POI364.

Bachmann, Ingrid, Dustin Harp, and Jamie Loke. 2018. "Covering Clinton (2010 – 2015): meaning-making strategies in US magazine covers." *Feminist Media Studies* 18 (5):793 – 809.

Back, Les. 2002. "Aryans reading Adorno: Cyber-culture and twenty-first-century racism." *Ethnic and Racial Studies* 25 (4):628 – 651. DOI: 10.1080/01419870220136664.

Baele, Stephane, and Lewys Brace. 2021. "Coalfax." *ExId Research Briefs* 1.

Bahrainwala, Lamiyah. 2021. "Shithole rhetorics." *Journal of International and Intercultural Communication* 14 (3):185 – 201.

Bail, Christopher. 2014. *Terrified: How Anti-Muslim Fringe Organizations Became Mainstream:* Princeton.

Bakhtin, Mikhail. 1968. *Rabelais and His World*, tr. Helene Iswolsky: MIT Press.

Bakhtin, Mikhail 2015. *Tvorchestvo Fransua Rable i narodnaya kul'tura srednevekov'ya i Renessansa:* Litres.

Ball, Arnetha F, Sarah Warshauer Freedman, and Roy Pea. 2004. *Bakhtinian Perspectives on Language, Literacy, and Learning:* Cambridge University Press.

Ball, Philip, and Amy Maxmen. 2020. "The epic battle against coronavirus misinformation and conspiracy theories." *Nature* 581 (7809):371 – 375.

Banet-Weiser, Sarah, and Jack Bratich. 2019. "From pick-up artists to incels: Con(fidence) games, networked misogyny, and the failure of neoliberalism." *International Journal of Communication* 13:1.

Banwart, Mary C, and Michael W Kearney. 2018. "Social dominance, sexism, and the lasting effects on political communication from the 2016 election." In *An Unprecedented Election: Media, Communication, and the Electorate in the 2016 Campaign*, 419–440. Praeger.

Bareau, Michel. 1987. *Les contes de Perrault, la contestation et ses limites furetière: Actes de Banff-1986; [le 18. congrès de la NASSCFL a tenu ses assises du 24 au 26 avril 1987, à Banff et au Lake Louise, en Alberta, Canada]*. Vol. 17: Papers on French Seventeenth Century Literature.

Barone, Michael. 2019. *How America's Political Parties Change (and How They Don't):* Encounter Books.

Barta, Peter I, Paul Allen Miller, Charles Platter, and David Shepherd. 2013. *Carnivalizing Difference: Bakhtin and the Other:* Routledge.

Bartlett, Jamie, Caterina Froio, Mark Littler, and Duncan McDonnell. 2013. "New political actors in Europe: Beppe Grillo and the M5S." *Demos Country Briefing Papers.*

Bastos, M, and J Farkas. 2019. "'Donald Trump is my President!': The internet research agency propaganda machine." *Social Media+ Society* 5 (3):2056305119865466.

Bauer, AJ. 2023. "Why so serious? Studying humor on the right." *Media, Culture & Society:*01634437231154779.

Baum, Matthew A. 2002. "Sex, lies, and war: How soft news brings foreign policy to the inattentive public." *American Political Science Review* 96 (1):91–109.

Baumgartner, Jody C. 2017. "Political humor, YouTube, and the 2016 presidential election." In *The Internet and the 2016 Presidential Campaign*, 219–238. Lexington Books.

Beauchamp, Zack. 2023. "'Soros-backed': The GOP's favorite attack on the man prosecuting Trump, explained." *VOX*, April 3. https://www.vox.com/23665035/trump-indictment-soros-backed-anti-semitism-george.

BBC News. 2020. "Trump retweets video of supporter shouting 'white power.'" June 28.

Becker, Amy B. 2020. "Trump trumps Baldwin? How Trump's tweets transform SNL into Trump's strategic advantage." *Journal of Political Marketing* 19 (4):386–404.

Beer, David, and Roger Burrows. 2010. *Consumption, Prosumption and Participatory Web Cultures: An Introduction.* Sage.

Benkler, Y, R Faris, and H Roberts. 2018. *Network Propaganda: Manipulation, Disinformation, and Radicalization in American Politics:* Oxford University Press.

Bennett, W Lance. 2015a. "Changing societies, changing media systems: Challenges for communication theory, research and education." In *Can the Media Serve Democracy ?*, 151–163. Springer.

Bennett, W Lance. 2015b. "Indexing theory." *The International Encyclopedia of Political Communication:*1–5.

Bennett, W Lance, and S Livingston. 2018. "The disinformation order: Disruptive communication and the decline of democratic institutions." *European Journal of Communication* 33 (2):122–139.

Bennett, W Lance, and Barbara Pfetsch. 2018. "Rethinking political communication in a time of disrupted public spheres." *Journal of Communication* 68 (2):243–253.

Bergen, M. (2019). "YouTube Executives Ignored Warnings, Letting Toxic Videos Run Rampant". *Bloomberg News.* 2 April 2019. https://www.bloomberg.com/news/features/2019-04-02/youtube-executives-ignored-warnings-letting-toxic-videos-run-rampant?leadSource=uverify%20wall.

Berger, Arthur Asa. 2016. "Marketing the president: Political marketing." In *Marketing and American Consumer Culture: A Cultural Studies Analysis*, 93–100. Palgrave Macmillan.

Berman, R. 2016. "Why are voters drawn to Donald Trump?" *The Atlantic*, April 8. http://www.the
   atlantic.com/politics/archive/2016/04/donald-trump-supporters-in-theirown-words/477396/.
Berntzen, Lars Erik. 2019. *Liberal Roots of Far Right Activism: The Anti-Islamic Movement in the 21st
   Century:* Routledge.
Billig, Michael. 2005. *Laughter and Ridicule: Towards a Social Critique of Humour:* Sage.
Blackledge, Adrian, and Angela Creese. 2014. "Heteroglossia as practice and pedagogy." In
   Heteroglossia as Practice and Pedagogy, 1–20. Springer.
Blake, A. 2016. "The final Trump-Clinton debate transcript, annotated." *The Washington Post*, October
   19. https://www.washingtonpost.com/news/the-fix/wp/2016/10/19/the-final-trump-clinton-debate-
   transcript-annotated/.
Blanchfield, Patrick. 2018. "Prosthetic gods: On the semiotic and affective landscape of firearms in
   American politics." In *Gun Studies*, 196–210. Routledge.
Bleakley, Paul. 2023. "Panic, pizza and mainstreaming the alt-right: A social media analysis of
   Pizzagate and the rise of the Qanon conspiracy." *Current Sociology* 71 (3):509–525.
Bleiker, Roland. 2016. *Visual Global Politics:* Routledge.
Boatright, Robert G, and Valerie Sperling. 2019. *Trumping Politics as Usual: Masculinity, Misogyny, and
   the 2016 Elections:* Oxford University Press.
Bogetić, K. (2023). Race and the language of incels: Figurative neologisms in an emerging English
   cryptolect. *English Today, 39*(2), 89–99.
Boje, David M. 2020. "Water avengers and their endgame." *Markets, Globalization & Development
   Review* 4 (4):6.
Bongino, Dan. 2020. *Follow the Money: The Shocking Deep State Connections of the Anti-Trump Cabal:*
   Post Hill Press.
Bonikowski, Bart, and Noam Gidron. 2016. "The populist style in American politics: Presidential
   campaign discourse, 1952–1996." *Social Forces* 94 (4):1593–1621.
Bordignon, Fabio, and Luigi Ceccarini. 2013. "Five stars and a cricket: Beppe Grillo shakes Italian
   politics." *South European Society and Politics* 18 (4):427–449.
Boxman-Shabtai, Lillian, and Limor Shifman. 2014. "Evasive targets: Deciphering polysemy in
   mediated humor." *Journal of Communication* 64 (5):977–998.
Boyarskaya, Natalia. 2015. "Roman et théorie, Boulgakov et Bakhtine: éclairages réciproques: Le
   Maître et Marguerite, le carnaval, la ménipée= Roman i teoriíà, Bulgakov i Bakhtin: vzaimnoe
   osveshchenie: Master i Margarita, karnaval, menippeĩà." Université de Lausanne, Faculté des
   lettres.
Boydstun, Amber E, and Regina G Lawrence. 2019. "When celebrity and political journalism collide:
   Reporting standards, entertainment, and the conundrum of covering Donald Trump's 2016
   campaign." *Perspectives on Politics:*1–16.
Braziel, Jana Evans, and Kathleen LeBesco. 2001. *Bodies Out of Bounds: Fatness and Transgression:*
   University of California Press.
Bristol, Michael D. 2014. *Carnival and Theater: Plebian Culture and The Structure of Authority in
   Renaissance England:* Routledge.
Brown, Jessica Autumn. 2016. "Running on fear: Immigration, race and crime framings in
   contemporary GOP presidential debate discourse." *Critical Criminology* 24 (3):315–331.
Brown, Katy, and Aurelien Mondon. 2021. "Populism, the media, and the mainstreaming of the far
   right: The Guardian's coverage of populism as a case study." *Politics* 41 (3):279–295.
Brownstein, Ronald. 2016. "Trump hardens America's divisions." *National Journal Daily.*

Brubaker, R. 2017. "Between nationalism and civilizationism: The European populist moment in comparative perspective." *Ethnic and Racial Studies* 40 (8):1191–1226.

Buckels, Erin E, Paul D Trapnell, and Delroy L Paulhus. 2014. "Trolls just want to have fun." *Personality and Individual Differences* 67:97–102.

Bucy, EP, JM Foley, J Lukito, L Doroshenko, DV Shah, JC Pevehouse, and C Wells. 2020. "Performing populism: Trump's transgressive debate style and the dynamics of Twitter response." *New Media & Society* 22 (4):634–658.

Burden, Barry C, Yoshikuni Ono, and Masahiro Yamada. 2017. "Reassessing public support for a female president." *The Journal of Politics* 79 (3):1073–1078.

Burke, Peter. 2005. "Performing history: The importance of occasions." *Rethinking History* 9 (1):35–52.

Burke, Peter. 1978. *Popular Culture in Early Modern Europe:* Harper & Row.

Byrd, Charles L. 1987. "Freud influence on Bakhtin, traces of psychoanalytic-theory in 'Rabelais and His World'." *Germano-Slavica* 5 (5–6):223–230.

Cameron, Deborah. 2020. "10 banter, male bonding, and the language of Donald Trump." In *Language in the Trump Era: Scandals and Emergencies*, 158–167. Cambridge University Press.

Campbell, Angus, Philip E Converse, Warren E Miller, and E Donald Stokes. 1960. *The American Voter:* University of Michigan Press.

Campbell, John W. 1996. "Professional wrestling: Why the bad guy wins." *Journal of American Culture* 19 (2):127–132.

Canella, Gino. 2016. "Occupy Raw: Pro wrestling fans, carnivalesque, and the commercialization of social movements." *The Journal of Popular Culture* 49 (6):1375–1392.

Canovan, Margaret. 1999. "Trust the people! Populism and the two faces of democracy." *Political Studies* 47 (1):2–16.

Carian, Emily K, Alex DiBranco, and Chelsea Ebin, eds. 2022. *Male Supremacism in the United States From Patriarchal Traditionalism to Misogynist Incels and the Alt-Right:* Routledge.

Carroll, Michael P. 1984. "The trickster as selfish-buffoon and culture hero." *Ethos* 12 (2):105–131.

Cay, William C. 1998. "The practice of linguistic nonviolence." *Peace Review* 10 (4):545–547.

Ceaser, James W. 2007. "Demagoguery, statesmanship, and the American presidency." *Critical Review* 19 (2–3):257–298.

Çelikkol, Askin. 2014. "Saturnalia revisited: Gezi Park protests and carnival today." *Cultura, lenguaje y representación: revista de estudios culturales de la Universitat Jaume I* 12:9–25.

Chattopadhyay, Swati, and Bhaskar Sarkar. 2005. "Introduction: The subaltern and the popular 1." *Postcolonial Studies* 8 (4):357–363.

Chouliaraki, Lilie. 2021. "Victimhood: The affective politics of vulnerability." *European Journal of Cultural Studies* 24 (1):10–27.

CJ. 2023. "NCGOP convention draws presidential primary frontrunners to make their case." *The Carolina Journal*, June 12. https://www.carolinajournal.com/ncgop-convention-draws-presidential-primary-frontrunners-to-make-their-case/.

Cluse, Christoph. 1995. "'Fabula ineptissima'. Die Ritualmordlegende um Adam von Bristol nach der Handschrift London, British Library, Harley 957." *Aschkenas: Zeitschrift für Geschichte und Kultur der Juden* 5 (2):293–330.

CNN Wire. 2015. "Donald Trump's 'blood' comment about Megyn Kelly backfires." August 8. https://www.wtvr.com/2015/08/08/donald-trumps-blood-comment-about-megyn-kelly-backfires.

Cohn, Carol. 1987. "Sex and death in the rational world of defense intellectuals." *Signs: Journal of Women in Culture and Society* 12 (4):687–718.

Cooper, Joel, and Joseph Avery. 2021. "Value framing and support for populist propaganda." In *The Psychology of Populism*, 319–331. Routledge.

Coronato, Rocco. 2003. *Jonson versus Bakhtin: Carnival and the Grotesque:* Rodopi.

Cotter, Michael. 2014. "New ways to express old hatred: The transformation of comic racism in British popular culture." Loughborough University.

Coveney, John, and William C Whit. 2000. "Food, morals and meaning: The pleasure and anxiety of eating." *Critical Public Health* 10 (4):467–467.

Cowan, Jane K. 1994. "Women, men and pre-Lenten carnival in northern Greece: An anthropological exploration of gender transformation in symbol and practice." *Rural History* 5 (2):195–210.

Cuccinello, Hayley C. 2016. "Trevor Noah's 'Daily Show' reaches 100th episode, but Noah is still struggling." *Forbes Magazine*, Apr il 28.

Cuen, L, and J Evers. 2016. "Donald Trump fans attack Megyn Kelly with sexist slurs." *Vocativ*, January 27.

Dahl, David. 2016. "Imagining the Monica Lewinsky scandal on social media." In *Scandal in a Digital Age*, 69–74. Palgrave Macmillan.

Dahlgren, Peter. 2003. "Reconfiguring civic culture in the new media milieu." In *Media and the Restyling of Politics*, 151–170. Sage.

Daniels, Jesse. 2009. *Cyber Racism: White Supremacy Online and the New Attack on Civil Rights:* Rowman & Littlefield.

Daniels, Jesse. 2018. "The algorithmic rise of the 'alt-right'." *Contexts* 17 (1):60–65.

Dann, Carrie. 2015. "Rick Perry unloads on Donald Trump's "barking carnival act."" *NBC News*, July 22. https://www.nbcnews.com/politics/2016-election/rick-perry-unloads-donald-trumps-barking-carnival-act-n396776.

Damon, Maria. 1997. "The Jewish entertainer as cultural lightning rod: The case of Lenny Bruce." *Postmodern Culture* 7 (2).

Danesi, Marcel. 2022. *Comedic Nightmare: The Trump Effect on American Comedy:* Brill.

Danow, David. 1995. *The Spirit of Carnival: Magical Realism and the Grotesque:* University Press of Kentucky.

Davis, Jenny L, Tony P Love, and Gemma Killen. 2018. "Seriously funny: The political work of humor on social media." *New Media & Society* 20 (10):3898–3916.

Dawsey, J. 2018. "Trump derides protections for immigrants from 'shithole' countries." *The Washington Post.* https://www.washingtonpost.com/politics/trump-attacks-protections-for-immigrants-from-shithole-countries-in-oval-office-meeting/2018/01/11/bfc0725c-f711-11e7-91af-31ac729add94_story.html.

Day, Benjamin S, and Alister Wedderburn. 2022. "Wrestlemania! Summit diplomacy and foreign policy performance after Trump." *International Studies Quarterly* 66 (2):sqac019.

De Gelder, Beatrice. 2006. "Towards the neurobiology of emotional body language." *Nature Reviews Neuroscience* 7 (3):242–249.

De Gelder, Beatrice, Josh Snyder, Doug Greve, George Gerard, and Nouchine Hadjikhani. 2004. "Fear fosters flight: A mechanism for fear contagion when perceiving emotion expressed by a whole body." *Proceedings of the National Academy of Sciences of the United States of America* 101 (47):16701–16706.

De Genova, Nicholas. n.d. "'Everything is permitted': Trump, white supremacy, fascism." American Anthropologist. https://www.americananthropologist.org/online-content/everything-is-permitted-trump-white-supremacy-fascism.

De Jonge, Léonie, and Elizaveta Gaufman. 2022. "The normalisation of the far right in the Dutch media in the run-up to the 2021 general elections." *Discourse & Society* 33 (6):773 – 787.

De Keulenaar, E, JC Magalhães, and B Ganesh. 2023. "Modulating moderation: A history of objectionability in Twitter moderation practices." *Journal of Communication* 73 (3):273 – 287.

Debord, G. 2021. *The Society of the Spectacle:* Unredacted Word.

Deem, Alexandra. 2019. "The digital traces of #whitegenocide and alt-right affective economies of transgression." *International Journal of Communication* 13:3183 – 3202.

Diaz, H. and Hecht-Felella, L. (2021). *Double Standards in Social Media Content Moderation*. New York: Brennan Center for Justice.

Díaz-Cintas, Jorge. 2018. "'Subtitling's a carnival': New practices in cyberspace." *Jostrans: The Journal of Specialised Translation* (30):127 – 149.

Dittmer, Jason. 2011. "American exceptionalism, visual effects, and the post-9/11 cinematic superhero boom." *Environment and Planning D: Society and Space* 29 (1):114 – 130.

Dittmer, Jason. 2016. "Captain America in the news: changing mediascapes and the appropriation of a superhero." In *Superheroes and Identities*, 245 – 260. Routledge.

Donnell, Alison. 2014. Review of *Island Bodies: Transgressive Sexualities in the Caribbean Imagination*, by Rosamond S King. *Caribbean Quarterly* 60 (4):122 – 124.

Donovan, Joan, Becca Lewis, and Brian Friedberg. 2019. "Parallel ports: Sociotechnical change from the alt-right to alt-tech." In *Post-digital Cultures of the Far Right*, 49 – 16. Transcript.

Douglas, Lawrence. 2020. "Paranoid politics: The malign myth of the American 'Deep State.'" *Times Literary Supplement* 6132 (October 9):21 – 22.

Drezner, Daniel W. 2020. *The Toddler in Chief: What Donald Trump Teaches Us about the Modern Presidency:* University of Chicago Press.

Ducat, Stephen J. 2005. *The Wimp Factor: Gender Gaps, Holy Wars, and the Politics of Anxious Masculinity:* Beacon Press.

Dulio, David A, and John S Klemanski. 2018. "Parties and Populism in 2016." In *American Political Parties Under Pressure: Strategic Adaptations for a Changing Electorate*, 43 – 75. Palgrave Macmillan.

Dupont, Benoit. 2008. "Hacking the panopticon: Distributed online surveillance and resistance." In *Surveillance and Governance: crime Control and Beyond*, 257 – 278. Emerald.

Dwyer, Colin. 2016. "Donald Trump: 'I could … shoot somebody, and I wouldn't lose any voters.'" *NPR*, January 23. https://www.npr.org/sections/thetwo-way/2016/01/23/464129029/donald-trump-i-could-shoot-somebody-and-i-wouldnt-lose-any-voters.

Eco, Umberto. 1984. "The frames of comic freedom." In *Carnival*, 1 – 9. Mouton.

Edelman, Murray. 1988. *Constructing the political spectacle:* University of Chicago Press.

Ekman, Mattias. 2015. "Online Islamophobia and the politics of fear: Manufacturing the green scare." *Ethnic and Racial Studies* 38 (11):1986 – 2002. https://doi.org/10.1080/01419870.2015.1021264.

Elias, Norbert, and Heike Hammer. 1979. *Über den prozess der zivilisation*. Vol. 2: Suhrkamp.

Elliot, Shanti. 1999. "Carnival and dialogue in Bakhtin's poetics of folklore." Folklore Forum.

Ellman, Michael. 2001. "The Soviet 1937 provincial show trials: Carnival or terror?" *Europe-Asia Studies* 53 (8):1221 – 1233.

Enders, Jody. 2004. "Theater makes history: Ritual murder by proxy in the Mistere de la Sainte Hostie." *Speculum* 79 (4):991 – 1016.

Enders, Jody. 2005. "Dramatic rumors and truthful appearances: The medieval myth of ritual murder by proxy." In *Rumor Mills: The Social Impact of Rumor and Legend*, 15 – 29. Routledge.

Erickson, Brad. 2021. "Grotesque logic: Catalan carnival utopias and the politics of laughter." *Visual Studies* 36 (4–5):507–523.

Erni, John Nguyet, and Ted Striphas. 2022. *The Cultural Politics of COVID-19:* Taylor & Francis.

Esser, Frank, and Barbara Pfetsch. 2004. *Comparing Political Communication: Theories, Cases, and Challenges:* Cambridge University Press.

Evans-Pritchard, Edward Evan. 1967. *The Zande Trickster:* Clarendon.

Evolvi, Giulia. 2018. "Hate in a tweet: Exploring internet-based Islamophobic discourses." *Religions* 9 (10):307. https://doi.org/10.3390/rel9100307.

Falasca, Kasja, Mikolaj Dymek, and Christina Grandien. 2019 "Social media election campaigning: Who is working for whom? A conceptual exploration of digital political labour." *Contemporary Social Science* 14 (1):89–101.

Farnsworth, Stephen J, and S Robert Lichter. 2019. *Late Night with Trump: Political Humor and the American Presidency:* Routledge.

Ferber, Abby. 1998. *White Man Falling: Race, Gender, and White Supremacy:* Rowman & Littlefield.

Fetissenko, Maxim. 2008. "Bakhtin's carnival as part of democratic elections: A re-examination." *Controversia* 6 (1):91–110.

Financial Times. 2023. Yevgeny Prigozhin, Wagner warlord, 1961–2023. Obituary. https://www.ft.com/content/34995fb5-07a9-4491-b94b-69b42ecda523.

Fisher, Marc, John Woodrow Cox, and Peter Hermann. 2016. "Pizzagate: From rumor, to hashtag, to gunfire in DC." *Washington Post* 6:8410–8415.

Fitzpatrick, Sheila. 2018. "How the mice buried the cat: Scenes from the Great Purges of 1937 in the Russian provinces." In *The Soviet Union*, 207–228. Routledge.

Foran, Clare. 2016. "Donald Trump's threats risk silencing women." Accessed November 7. http://www.theatlantic.com/politics/archive/2016/10/trump-women-sexual-assault/504446/.

Fording, Richard C, and Sanford F Schram. 2020. *Hard White: The Mainstreaming of Racism in American Politics:* Oxford University Press.

Foucault, Michel. 1977. *Discipline and Punish: The Birth of the Prison:* Vintage.

Fox, Stuart. 2013. "Is it time to update the definition of political participation?" *Parliamentary Affairs* 67 (2):495–505.

Frazer, James George. 2012 *The Golden Bough:* Cambridge University Press.

Freelon, Deen, Michael Bossetta, Chris Wells, Josephine Lukito, Yiping Xia, and Kirsten Adams. 2022. "Black trolls matter: Racial and ideological asymmetries in social media disinformation." *Social Science Computer Review* 40 (3):560–578.

Gambarato, Renira R. 2012. "Signs, systems and complexity of transmedia storytelling." *Estudos em Comunicação* 12 (1):69–83.

Ganesh, Bharath. 2018. "The ungovernability of digital hate culture." *Journal of International Affairs* 71 (2):30–49.

Ganesh, Bharath. 2020. "Weaponizing white thymos: Flows of rage in the online audiences of the alt-right." *Cultural Studies* 34 (6):892–924.

Ganesh, Bharath, and Caterina Froio. 2020. "A 'Europe des Nations': Far right imaginative geographies and the politicization of cultural crisis on Twitter in Western Europe." *Journal of European Integration* 42 (5):715–732.

Ganesh, B. (2021). "Platform Racism: How Minimizing Racism Privileges Far Right Extremism". *SSRC Items*. 16 March 2021. https://items.ssrc.org/extremism-online/platform-racism-how-minimizing-racism-privileges-far-right-extremism/.

Gardiner, Michael E, and Michael Mayerfeld Bell. 1998. *Bakhtin and the Human Sciences: No Last Words:* Sage.

Garland, David. 2005. "Penal excess and surplus meaning: Public torture lynchings in twentieth-century America." *Law & Society Review* 39 (4):793–834.

Gaufman, Elizaveta. 2017. "Sexuality must be defended." In *Security Threats and Public Perception*, 145–165. Palgrave Macmillan.

Gaufman, Elizaveta. 2022. "Damsels in distress: Fragile masculinity in digital war." *Media, War & Conflict:*17506352221130271.

Gaufman, Elizaveta. 2023. "Trump's the man." In *Everyday Foreign Policy*, 84–100. Manchester University Press.

Gerbaudo, P. 201 9. *The Digital Party: Political Organisation and Online Democracy:* Pluto Press.

Gilbert, Christopher J. 2019. "Alec Baldwin as Donald Trump on Saturday Night Live." In *Routledge Handbook of Character Assassination and Reputation Management*, 209–224. Routledge.

Gilhus, Ingvild Salid. 1990. "Carnival in religion: The Feast of Fools in France." *Numen* 37 (Fasc. 1):24–52.

Gilman, Sander L. 2019. *Disease and Representation: Images of Illness from Madness to AIDS:* Cornell University Press.

Gilmore, David D. 2010. *Misogyny: The Male Malady:* University of Pennsylvania Press.

Ging, Debbie, and Eugenia Siapera. 2019. *Gender Hate Online: Understanding the New Anti-feminism:* Springer.

Ginsburg, Ruth. 1993. "The pregnant text: Bakhtin's ur-chronotope: The womb." *Critical Studies* 3 (2):165–176.

Giroux, Henry A. 2019. "Neoliberalism and the weaponising of language and education." *Race & class* 61 (1):26–45.

Giroux, Henry A. 2022. *Fascism on Trial: Rethinking Education in an Age of Conspiracy Theories and Election Deniers:* Taylor & Francis.

Gökarıksel, Banu, and Sara Smith. 2017. "Intersectional feminism beyond US flag hijab and pussy hats in Trump's America." *Gender, Place & Culture* 24 (5):628–644.

Golkar, Saeid. 2011. "Liberation or suppression technologies? The Internet, the Green Movement and the regime in Iran." *International Journal of Emerging Technologies and Society* 9 (1):50.

Gothard, Kelly Caroline. 2021. *The Incel Lexicon: Deciphering the Emergent Cryptolect of a Global Misogynistic Community:* The University of Vermont and State Agricultural College.

Gottfried, Jeffrey, Michael Barthel, Elisa Shearer, and Amy Mitchell. 2016. "The 2016 presidential campaign: A news event that's hard to miss." Pew Research Center, February 4. https://www.pe wresearch.org/journalism/2016/02/04/the-2016-presidential-campaign-a-news-event-thats-hard-to-miss/.

Gottfried, J, and E Shearer. 2016. "News use across social media platforms 2016." Pew Research Center. https://apo.org.au/node/64483.

Graber, D, and James Smith. 2005. "Political communication faces the 21st century." *Journal of Communication* 55 (3):479–507.

Graham, Bryan Armen. 2017. "Donald Trump blasts NFL anthem protesters: 'Get that son of a bitch off the field.'" *The Guardian*, September 23. https://www.theguardian.com/sport/2017/sep/22/donald-trump-nfl-national-anthem-protests.

Graham, Lucy Valerie. 2020. "On misogyny and the women who say 'no'." *Safundi* 21 (4):416–432.

Graham, Seth Benedict. 2003. "A cultural analysis of the Russo-Soviet anekdot." University of Pittsburgh.

Gray, R. 2017. "Trump defends white-nationalist protesters: 'Some very fine people on both sides.'" *The Atlantic*, August 15. https://www.theatlantic.com/politics/archive/2017/08/trump-defends-white-nationalist-protesters-some-very-fine-people-on-both-sides/537012/.

Greene, Doyle. 2018. "Will the real Omarosa please stand up? CBS and the spectacle of Trumpism." *Film Criticism* 42 (4).

Grinshteyn, A. 2000. "Karnaval i maskarad: dva tipa kul'tury." *"Na granitsakh". Zarubezhnaya literatura ot srednevekov'ya do sovremennosti. Sb. statey/otv. red. LG Andreyev. M.: Izd-vo Mosk. un-ta:*22–43.

Groys, Boris. 2017. "Between Stalin and Dionysus: Bakhtin's theory of the carnival." *Dialogic Pedagogy: An International Online Journal* 5.

Gürel, EMET, and Ö Tığlı. 2014. "New world created by social media: Transmedia storytelling." *Journal of Media Critiques. Special Issue* 1:35–65.

Hagen, William W. 2005. "The moral economy of ethnic violence: The pogrom in Lwow, November 1918." *Geschichte und Gesellschaft* 31 (2):203–226.

Hall, Kira, Donna M Goldstein, and Matthew Bruce Ingram. 2016. "The hands of Donald Trump: Entertainment, gesture, spectacle." *HAU: Journal of Ethnographic Theory* 6 (2):71–100.

Hall, Stuart, and Allon White. 1993. *Carnival, Hysteria, and Writing:* Clarendon Press.

Haney-López, Ian. 2014. *Dog Whistle Politics: How Coded Racial Appeals Have Reinvented Racism and Wrecked the Middle Class:* Oxford University Press.

Hansen, Lene. 2011. "The politics of securitization and the Muhammad cartoon crisis: A post-structuralist perspective." *Security Dialogue* 42 (4–5):357–369.

Hardaker, Claire. 2010. "Trolling in asynchronous computer-mediated communication: From user discussions to academic definitions." *Journal of Politeness Research* 6 (2):161–182.

Harold, Christine, and Kevin Michael DeLuca. 2005. "Behold the corpse: Violent images and the case of Emmett Till." *Rhetoric & Public Affairs* 8 (2):263–286.

Harp, Dustin. 2019. *Gender in the 2016 US Presidential Election: Trump, Clinton, and Media Discourse:* Routledge.

Harris, Max. 2003. *Carnival and Other Christian Festivals: Folk Theology and Folk Performance:* University of Texas Press.

Harris, Max. 2011. *Sacred Folly: A New History of the Feast of Fools:* Cornell University Press.

Hart, Roderick P. 2013. "The rhetoric of political comedy: A tragedy?" *International Journal of Communication* 7:338–370.

Hawley, George. 2017. *Making Sense of the Alt-right:* Columbia University Press.

Heidt, Stephen J. 2018. "Scapegoater-in-Chief: Racist undertones of Donald Trump's rhetorical repertoire." In *The Trump Presidency, Journalism, and Democracy*, 206–228. Routledge.

Hirschkop, Ken. 1986. "Bakhtin, discourse and democracy." *New Left Review* (160):92.

Hochschild, Arlie Russell. 2018. *Strangers in Their Own Land: Anger and Mourning on the American Right:* The New Press.

Hofstadter, Richard. 1963. *Anti-intellectualism in American Life:* Vintage.

Holloway, Julian, and James Kneale. 2002. "Mikhail Bakhtin: Dialogics of space." In *Thinking Space*, 84–94. Routledge.

Hopper, Nate. 2016. "Why you shouldn't laugh at Donald Trump's hands." *TIME Magazine*, October 20. https://time.com/4539487/donald-trump-small-hands/.

Howard, Philip N, Samuel Woolley, and Ryan Calo. 2018. "Algorithms, bots, and political communication in the US 2016 election: The challenge of automated political communication for election law and administration." *Journal of Information Technology & Politics* 15 (2):81–93.

Howard, Philip SS. 2018. "On the back of blackness: Contemporary Canadian blackface and the consumptive production of post-racialist, white Canadian subjects." *Social Identities* 24 (1):87–103.

Hoy, Mikita. 1994. "Joyful mayhem: Bakhtin, football songs, and the carnivalesque." *Text and Performance Quarterly* 14 (4):289–304.

Hughes, Geoffrey. 2011. *Political Correctness: A History of Semantics and Culture:* John Wiley & Sons.

Humphrey, Chris. 2000. "Bakhtin and the study of popular culture: Re-thinking carnival as a historical and analytical concept." In *Materializing Bakhtin*, 164–172. Springer.

Humphreys, Ashlee, and Kent Grayson. 2008. "The intersecting roles of consumer and producer: A critical perspective on co-production, co-creation and prosumption." *Sociology Compass* 2 (3):963–980.

Inwood, Joshua. 2019. "White supremacy, white counter-revolutionary politics, and the rise of Donald Trump." *Environment and Planning C: Politics and Space* 37 (4):579–596.

Ivaldi, Gilles, and Maria Elisabetta Lanzone. 2016. "The French Front National: Organizational change and adaptation from Jean-Marie to Marine Le Pen." In *Understanding Populist Party Organisation: The Radical Right in Western Europe*, 131–158. Palgrave Macmillan.

Jackson, Robert. 2008. "A southern sublimation: Lynching film and the reconstruction of American memory." *The Southern Literary Journal* 40 (2):102–120.

Jaffe, Alexandra. 2016. "Donald Trump has 'small hands,' Marco Rubio says." *NBC News*, February 29. https://www.nbcnews.com/politics/2016-election/donald-trump-has-small-hands-marco-rubio-says-n527791.

James, Aaron. 2016. "On the philosophical interest and surprising significance of the asshole." *The Harvard Review of Philosophy* 23.

Jamison, Peter. 2022. "The angry white populist who paved the way for Trump." *Washington Post*, May 19. https://www.washingtonpost.com/history/interactive/2022/george-wallace-trump-white-anger/.

Janack, James A. 2005. *Vladimir Zhirinovsky: The Clown Prince of Russia:* Controversia.

Janack, James A. 2006. "The rhetoric of "the body:" Jesse Ventura and Bakhtin's carnival." *Communication Studies* 57 (2):197–214.

Jenkins, Henry. 2010. "Transmedia storytelling and entertainment: An annotated syllabus." *Continuum* 24 (6):943–958.

Jimenez, Mary Ann. 1997. "Gender and psychiatry: Psychiatric conceptions of mental disorders in women, 1960–1994." *Affilia* 12 (2):154–175.

Jones, Chris. 2017. "Alec Baldwin gets under Trump's skin: Comedy and tragedy in an age of political chaos." *The Atlantic* 319 (4):46–59.

Kallis, Aristotle. 2007. "'Licence' and genocide in the East: Reflections on localised eliminationist violence during the first stages of 'Operation Barbarossa' (1941)." *Studies in Ethnicity and Nationalism* 7 (3):6–23.

Kallis, Aristotle. 2008. *Genocide and Fascism: The Eliminationist Drive in Fascist Europe:* Routledge.

Kallis, Aristotle. 2013. "Far-right 'contagion' or a failing 'mainstream' ? How dangerous ideas cross borders and blur boundaries." *Democracy and Security* 9 (3):221–246.

Kaltwasser, Cristóbal Rovira, and Paul Taggart. 2016. "Dealing with populists in government: A framework for analysis." *Democratization* 23 (2):201–220.

Kang, Cecelia. 2016. "Fake news onslaught targets pizzeria as nest of child-trafficking." *The New York Times*, November 21.

Karpf, David. 2017. "Digital politics after Trump." *Annals of the International Communication Association* 41 (2):198–207.

Katz, Elihu. 1987. "Communications research since Lazarsfeld." *The Public Opinion Quarterly* 51:S25-S45.

Keller, Tobias R, and Ulrike Klinger. 2019. "Social bots in election campaigns: Theoretical, empirical, and methodological implications." *Political Communication* 36 (1):171–189.

Kelly, Casey Ryan. 2018. "Emasculating Trump: Incredulity, homophobia, and the spectacle of white masculinity." *QED: A Journal in GLBTQ Worldmaking* 5 (3):1–27.

Kelly, Casey Ryan, and Chase Aunspach. 2020. "Incels, compulsory sexuality, and fascist masculinity." *Feminist Formations* 32 (3):145–172.

Kelly, Catriona. 1990. *Petrushka: The Russian carnival puppet theatre:* Cambridge University Press.

Kennedy, Rodney Wallace. 2021. *The Immaculate Mistake: How Evangelicals Gave Birth to Donald Trump:* Wipf and Stock.

Kim, Young Mie, Jordan Hsu, David Neiman, Colin Kou, Levi Bankston, Soo Yun Kim, Richard Heinrich, Robyn Baragwanath, and Garvesh Raskutti. 2018. "The stealth media? Groups and targets behind divisive issue campaigns on Facebook." *Political Communication* 35 (4):515–541.

Kirby, Elia E. 2004. "CarnyLand (an ethnography): A study of contemporary carnivals and carnival workers (carnies) in British Columbia." University of British Columbia.

Kivisto, Peter. 2019. "The politics of cruelty." *The Sociological Quarterly* 60 (2):191–200.

Klikauer, Thomas, and Nadine Campbell. 2020. "Our toddler in chief: Trump rules by temper tantrums and bullying." *BuzzFlash.*

Klimmt, Christoph, Peter Vorderer, and Ute Ritterfeld. 2007. "Interactivity and generalizability: New media, new challenges." *Communication Methods and Measures* 1 (3):169–179.

Klinger, Ulrike, and Jakob Svensson. 2015. "The emergence of network media logic in political communication: A theoretical approach." *New Media & Society* 17 (8):1241–1257.

Klumbyte, Neringa. 2012. "Soviet ethical citizenship: Morality, the state, and laughter in late Soviet Lithuania." In *Communism Unwrapped*, 91–116. Oxford University Press.

Knopf, Christina M. 2021. *Politics in the Gutters: American Politicians and Elections in Comic Book Media:* University Press of Mississippi.

Kolehmainen, Pekka. 2017. "Social media narratives as political fan fiction in the 2016 US presidential election." *European Journal of American Studies* 12 (2).

Kolyazin, Vladimir. 2002. *Ot misterii k karnavalu: Teatral'nost' nemetskoy religioznoy i ploshchadnoy stseny rannego i pozdnego srednevekov'ya:* Федеральное государственное унитарное предприятие Академический научно ....

Komins, Benton Jay. 2001. "Western culture and the ambiguous legacies of the pig." *CLCWeb: Comparative Literature and Culture* 3 (4):6.

Kopan, Tal. 2016. "Donald Trump retweets 'White Genocide' Twitter user." *CNN*, January 16. https://edition.cnn.com/2016/01/22/politics/donald-trump-retweet-white-genocide/index.html.

Koplatadze, Tamar. 2019. "Theorising Russian postcolonial studies." *Postcolonial Studies* 22 (4):469–489.

Koul, Scaachi. 2018. "Why calling Ivanka Trump a 'feckless cunt' misses the mark." *BuzzFeed News*, June 1. https://www.buzzfeednews.com/article/scaachikoul/samantha-bee-feckless-cunt-ivanka-trump.

Kristeva, Julia. 1982. *Powers of Horror:* University Presses of California, Columbia and Princeton.

Kristeva, Julia. 2000. "Bakhtin, Slovo, dialog, Roman." *Vestnik MGU* 9:97–124.

Kruikemeier, Sanne, Guda Van Noort, Rens Vliegenthart, and Claes H De Vreese. 2013. "Getting closer: The effects of personalized and interactive online political communication." *European Journal of Communication* 28 (1):53–66.

Krystalli, Roxani. 2019. "'We are not good victims': Hierarchies of suffering and the politics of victimhood in Colombia." Tufts University.

Krystalli, Roxani C. 2021. "Narrating victimhood: Dilemmas and (in) dignities." *International Feminist Journal of Politics* 23 (1):125–146.

Kuipers, Giselinde. 2008. "The sociology of humor." *The Primer of Humor Research* 8:361–398.

Kumar, Deepa. 2012. *Islamophobia and the Politics of Empire:* Haymarket Books.

Kundnani, Arun. 2014. *The Muslims are Coming!: Islamophobia, Extremism, and the Domestic War on Terror:* Verso Books.

Kunemund, Adrian. 2019. "The role of sexism in white heterosexual women's voting behaviors in the 2016 presidential election: A feminist perspective." University of Georgia.

Lacatus, Corina, and Gustav Meibauer. 2022. "'Saying it like it is': Right-wing populism, international politics, and the performance of authenticity." *The British Journal of Politics and International Relations* 24 (3):437–457.

Laineste, Liisi. 2008. *Post-socialist Jokes in Estonia: Continuity and Change:* Tartu University Press.

Lajevardi, Nazita, and Kassra AR Oskooii. "Old-fashioned racism, contemporary Islamophobia, and the isolation of Muslim Americans in the age of Trump." *Journal of Race, Ethnicity, and Politics* 3 (1):112–152.

Langer, Armin. 2022. "Dog-whistle politics as a strategy of American nationalists and populists: George Soros, the Rothschilds, and other conspiracy theories." In *Nationalism and Populism: Expressions of Fear or Political Strategies?*, 157–187. De Gruyter.

Lee, Han Soo. 2014. "Analyzing the multidirectional relationships between the president, news media, and the public: Who affects whom?" *Political Communication* 31 (2):259–281.

Leidig, E. (2023). *The Women of the Far Right: Social Media Influencers and Online Radicalization.* Columbia University Press.

Leonardo, Cecilia, and Joan C Chrisler. 1992. "Women and sexually transmitted diseases." *Women & Health* 18 (4):1–15.

Lewis, Rebecca. 2018. *Alternative Influence: Broadcasting the Reactionary Right on YouTube:* Data & Society.

Lewis, Rebecca. 2020. "'This is what the news won't show you': YouTube creators and the reactionary politics of micro-celebrity." *Television & New Media* 21 (2):201–217.

Lindahl, Carl. 1996. "Bakhtin's carnival laughter and the Cajun country Mardi Gras." *Folklore* 107 (1–2):57–70.

Linvill, Darren L, and Patrick L Warren. 2020. "Troll factories: Manufacturing specialized disinformation on Twitter." *Political Communication* 37 (4):447–467.

Lock, Charles. 1991. "Carnival and incarnation: Bakhtin and orthodox theology." *Literature and Theology* 5 (1):68–82.

Lockett, Alexandria. 2021. "What is Black Twitter? A rhetorical criticism of race, dis/information, and social media." In *Race, Rhetoric, and Research Methods*, 165–213. University Press of Colorado.

Löfflmann, Georg. 2022. "'Enemies of the people': Donald Trump and the security imaginary of America First." *The British Journal of Politics and International Relations* 24 (3):543–560.

Lopez, German. 2016. "Republicans: Where did Donald Trump come from? The Daily Show: You created him." *Vox*, March 24. https://www.vox.com/2016/3/24/11297512/daily-show-trump-republicans.

Lopez, German. 2017. "Stephen Colbert responds to outcry over homophobic anti-Trump joke: 'I would change a few words.'" *Vox*, May 4. https://www.vox.com/culture/2017/5/4/15542148/stephen-colbert-firecolbert-homophobic-late-show.

Lott, Eric. 2013. *Love & Theft: Blackface Minstrelsy and the American Working Class:* Oxford University Press.

Luddy, Cian. 2021. "Going coronaviral: Trump, Twitter and the (de) securitization of COVID-19." Paper presented at Pandemic Tech: The Interplay of Covid-19 and Technology in Shaping the Pandemic Experience. Belfast.

Lukito, Josephine. 2019. "Coordinating a multi-platform disinformation campaign: Internet research agency activity on three US social media platforms, 2015 to 2017." *Political Communication*:1–18.

Luthar, Breda. 2023. "Celebrity and the displacement of class." In *The Cultural Politics of Anti-Elitism*, 263–282. Routledge.

Luthin, Reinhard H. 1951. "Some demagogues in American history." *The American Historical Review* 57 (1):22–46.

Macdonald, Dwight. 2006. "Masscult and midcult." In *Popular Culture Theory and Methodology: A Basic Introduction*, 9–14. University of Wisconsin Press.

Machkovech, S. 2016. "Facebook apologises for feeding inflated video-view numbers to advertisers." *The New York Times*, September 23.

Mahdawi, Arwa. 2018. "Samantha Bee proves there's still one word you cannot say in America." The Guardian, June 2. https://www.theguardian.com/tv-and-radio/2018/jun/01/samantha-bee-ivanka-trump-c-word-america.

Malmqvist, Karl. 2015. "Satire, racist humour and the power of (un) laughter: On the restrained nature of Swedish online racist discourse targeting EU-migrants begging for money." *Discourse & Society* 26 (6):733–753.

Mandell, Hinda. 2019. *Crafting Dissent: Handicraft as Protest from the American Revolution to the Pussyhats:* Rowman & Littlefield.

Marquardt, Joachim. 1963. "Das Sakralwesen." In *Römische Staatsverwaltung* 3 (3).

Martin, John D. 2006. "The depiction of Jews in the carnival plays and comedies of Hans Folz and Hans Sachs in early modern Nuremberg." *Baylor Journal of Theatre and Performance* 3 (2):43–65.

Martin, Keir, and Jakob Krause-Jensen. 2017. "Trump: Transacting trickster." *Anthropology Today* 33 (3):5–8.

Martínez, Jessica, and Gregory A Smith. 2016. "How the faithful voted: A preliminary 2016 analysis." Pew Research Center. November 9. https://www.pewresearch.org/fact-tank/2016/11/09/how-the-faithful-voted-a-preliminary-2016-analysis/.

Marvin, Carolyn. 1994. "Fresh blood, public meat rituals of totem regeneration in the 1992 presidential race." *Communication Research* 21 (3):264–292.

Marvin, Carolyn, and David W Ingle. 1999. *Blood Sacrifice and the Nation: Totem Rituals and the American Flag:* Cambridge University Press.

Mason, Lilliana. 2018. *Uncivil Agreement: How Politics Became Our Identity:* University of Chicago Press.

Massanari, Adrienne. 2017. "# Gamergate and the Fappening: How Reddit's algorithm, governance, and culture support toxic technocultures." *New Media & Society* 19 (3):329–346.

Massoumi, Narzanin, Tom Mills, and David Miller. 2017. *What Is Islamophobia?: Racism, Social Movements and the State:* Pluto Press.

Matamoros-Fernández, Ariadna. 2020. "'El Negro de WhatsApp' meme, digital blackface, and racism on social media." *First Monday* 25 (1).

Mathewson, Dan. 2018. "Redneck rebel, the governor, and the Syrian sheik: Small town wrestling in the poor white south." *The Popular Culture Studies Journal* 6 (1):283–297.

Mathis-Lilley, Ben. 2016 "Donald Trump alluded to the size of his penis at the Republican debate." *The Slate.* March 3. http://www.slate.com/blogs/the_slatest/2016/03/03/donald_trump_penis_size_i_can_t_believe_i_m_writing_this.html.

May, Rob, and Matthew Feldman. 2019. "Understanding the alt-right: Ideologues, 'Lulz' and hiding in plain sight." In *Post-Digital Cultures of the Far Right*, 25–36. Transcript.

Mazzoleni, Gianpietro, and Winfried Schulz. 1999. "'Mediatization' of politics: A challenge for democracy?" *Political Communication* 16 (3):247–261.

McCaron, Meghan (2019) This is what democracy tastes like. Eater December 9, 2019. https://www.eater.com/2019/12/9/20992394/election-2020-eating-biden-sanders-warren-buttigieg-politicians-diners.

McCarty, Nolan, Keith T Poole, and Howard Rosenthal. 2016. *Polarized America: The Dance of Ideology and Unequal Riches:* MIT Press.

McDonald, Nicola. 2014. *Medieval Obscenities:* Boydell & Brewer.

McVeigh, Rory, and Kevin Estep. 2020. *The Politics of Losing: Trump, the Klan, and the Mainstreaming of Resentment:* Columbia University Press.

Meier, Matthew. 2020. "Trump vs. comedy: The carnivalesque politics of late-night." In *Laughter, Outrage and Resistance: Post-Trump TV Satire in Political Discourse and Dissent*, 7–26. Peter Lang.

Mendes, Amy E. 2016. "Digital demagogue: The critical candidacy of Donald J. Trump." *Journal of Contemporary Rhetoric* 6 (3/4):62–73.

Merrin, William. 2019. "President troll: Trump, 4chan and memetic warfare." In *Trump's Media War*, 201–226. Springer.

Meyer, Matthew. 2016. "Assholes: A theory of Donald Trump." *The Philosophers' Magazine* (75):109–111.

Milbrath, Lester W, and Madan Lal Goel. 1977. *Political Participation: How and Why Do People Get Involved in Politics?:* Rand McNally College Pub.

Miller, Arthur H. 1999. "Sex, politics, and public opinion: What political scientists really learned from the Clinton-Lewinsky scandal." *PS: Political Science & Politics* 32 (4):721–729.

Miller-Idriss, Cynthia. 2018. *The Extreme Gone Mainstream: Commercialization and Far Right Youth Culture in Germany:* Princeton University Press.

Miller-Idriss, Cynthia. 2020. *Hate in the Homeland: The New Global Far Right:* Princeton University Press.

Minchenia, Alena, Barbara Törnquist-Plewa, and Yuliya Yurchuk. 2018. "Humour as a mode of hegemonic control: Comic representations of Belarusian and Ukrainian leaders in official Russian media." In *Cultural and Political Imaginaries in Putin's Russia*, 211–231. Brill.

Mocanu, Delia, Luca Rossi, Qian Zhang, Marton Karsai, and Walter Quattrociocchi. 2015. "Collective attention in the age of (mis) information." *Computers in Human Behavior* 51:1198–1204.

Moody-Ramirez, Mia, and Andrew B Church. 2019. "Analysis of Facebook meme groups used during the 2016 US presidential election." *Social Media+ Society* 5 (1):2056305118808799.

Moon, David S. 2022. "Kayfabe, smartdom and marking out: Can pro-wrestling help us understand Donald Trump?" *Political Studies Review* 20 (1):47–61.

Morozov, Evgeny. 2011. *The Net Delusion: How Not to Liberate the World:* Penguin.

Morozov, Viatcheslav. 2015. *Russia's Postcolonial Identity: A Subaltern Empire in a Eurocentric World:* Palgrave Macmillan.

Morrison, Toni. 2016. "Aftermath: Sixteen writers on Trump's America." *The New Yorker*, November 13. https://www.newyorker.com/magazine/2016/11/21/aftermath-sixteen-writers-on-trumps-amer ica.

Morson, Gary Saul, and Caryl Emerson. 1990. *Mikhail Bakhtin: Creation of a Prosaics:* Stanford University Press.

Moscow Times. 2022. "Russian church leader appears to blame gay pride parades for Ukraine War." March 7. https://www.themoscowtimes.com/2022/03/07/russian-church-leader-appears-to-blame-gay-pride-parades-for-ukraine-war-a76803.

Moshin, Jamie. 2018. "Hello darkness: Antisemitism and rhetorical silence in the 'Trump Era'." *Journal of Contemporary Rhetoric* 8 (1/2):26 – 43.

Moy, Patricia, Michael A Xenos, and Verena K Hess. 2005. "Priming effects of late-night comedy." *International Journal of Public Opinion Research* 18 (2):198 – 210.

Mudde, Cas. 2004. "The populist zeitgeist." *Government and Opposition* 39 (4):541 – 563.

Mudde, Cas. 2017. "Populism: An ideational approach." In *The Oxford Handbook of Populism*, 27 – 47. Oxford University Press.

Mudde, Cas. 2020. *The Far Right Today:* Polity Press.

Mukhopadhyay, Bhaskar. 2004. "Between elite hysteria and subaltern carnivalesque: The politics of street-food in the city of Calcutta." *South Asia Research* 24 (1):37 – 50.

Murphy, Peter F. 2006. "Living by his wits: The buffoon and male survival." *Signs: Journal of Women in Culture and Society* 31 (4):1125 – 1142.

Murphy, Richard John. 1999. *Theorizing the Avant-Garde: Modernism, Expressionism, and the Problem of Postmodernity:* Cambridge University Press.

Nagle, Angela. 2017. *Kill All Normies: Online Culture Wars from 4chan and Tumblr to Trump and the Alt-Right:* John Hunt Publishing.

Nededog, Jethro and Skye Gould. 2017. "Who's winning and losing late-night TV under Trump." *Business Insider*, March 10. https://www.businessinsider.com/late-night-show-tv-ratings-under-trump-2017-3.

Nell, Sharon Diane. 2001. "The last laugh: Carnivalizing the feminine in Piron's 'La puce'." In *Carnivalizing Difference: Bakhtin and the Other*, 165 – 190. Routledge.

Nelson, L. 2016 "Trump kicks off 'birther' press spectacle by promoting his hotel." *Politico*, September 16. http://www.politico.com/story/2016/09/trump-hotel-birther-press-conference-228279.

Noble, Safiya Umoja. 2018. *Algorithms of Oppression: How Search Engines Reinforce Racism:* NYU Press.

Noel, Samantha A. 2010. "De jamette in we: Redefining performance in contemporary Trinidad carnival." *Small Axe: A Caribbean Journal of Criticism* 14 (1):60 – 78.

Noor, Poppy. 2019. "Trump posted a picture of himself as Rocky: No one knows what to make of it." *The Guardian*, November 27. https://www.theguardian.com/us-news/2019/nov/27/donald-trump-rocky-picture-twitter?CMP=Share_iOSApp_Other.

Norris, Pippa, and Ronald Inglehart. 2019. *Cultural Backlash: Trump, Brexit, and Authoritarian Populism:* Cambridge University Press.

North, Anna. 2019. "Why the president is feuding with Megan Rapinoe, star of the US women's soccer team." *Vox*, July 3. https://www.vox.com/identities/2019/7/3/20680073/megan-rapinoe-trump-world-cup-soccer.

O'Callaghan, D., Greene, D., Conway, M., Carthy, J., & Cunningham, P. (2015). Down the (White) Rabbit Hole: The Extreme Right and Online Recommender Systems. *Social Science Computer Review*, 33(4), 459 – 478. https://doi.org/10.1177/0894439314555329

Ostiguy, Pierre. 2017. "A socio-cultural approach." In *The Oxford Handbook of Populism*, 73–97. Oxford University Press.

Ostiguy, Pierre, Francisco Panizza, and Benjamin Moffitt. 2021. *Populism in Global Perspective: A Performative and Discursive Approach:* Routledge.

Otero, Solimar. 1996. "'Fearing our mothers': An overview of the psychoanalytic theories concerning the 'vagina dentata' motif F547. 1.1." *American Journal of Psychoanalysis* 56 (3):269–288.

Outar, Lisa. 2017. "Indigenous sexualities: Rosamond S. King's Island Bodies and the radical politics of scholarship." *Small Axe: A Caribbean Journal of Criticism* 21 (1):241–249.

Padilla, Yajaira M. 2022. *From Threatening Guerillas to Forever Illegals: US Central Americans and the Cultural Politics of Non-Belonging:* University of Texas Press.

Paltemaa, Lauri, and Juha A Vuori. 2009. "Regime transition and the Chinese politics of technology: From mass science to the controlled internet." *Asian Journal of Political Science* 17 (1):1–23.

Pan'kov, N A. 2010. *Voprosy biografii i nauchnogo tvorchestva M. M. Bakhtina:* Izd-vo MGU.

Parks, Perry. 2019. "Covering Trump's 'carnival': A rhetorical alternative to 'objective' reporting." *Journalism Practice*:1–21.

Parmar, Inderjeet. 2012. "US presidential election 2012: Post-truth politics." *Political Insight* 3 (2):4–7.

Parsons, Adam. 2022. "Italy will move to the right, the question is just how far." *Sky News*, September 26. https://news.sky.com/story/italy-will-move-to-the-right-the-question-is-just-how-far-12705513.

Pearce, Katy, and Adnan Hajizada. 2014. "No laughing matter: Humor as a means of dissent in the digital era: The case of authoritarian Azerbaijan." *Demokratizatsiya* 22 (1):67–85.

Pearson, Elizabeth. 2018. "Online as the new frontline: Affect, gender, and ISIS-take-down on social media." *Studies in Conflict & Terrorism* 41 (11):850–874.

Pengelly, Martin. 2019. "'Go back home': Trump aims racist attack at Ocasio-Cortez and other congresswomen." *The Guardian*, July 15. https://www.theguardian.com/us-news/2019/jul/14/trump-squad-tlaib-omar-pressley-ocasio-cortez.

Pérez, Raúl. 2022. *The Souls of White Jokes: How Racist Humor Fuels White Supremacy:* Stanford University Press.

Pérez, Raúl, and Geoff Ward. 2019. "From insult to estrangement and injury: The violence of racist police jokes." *American Behavioral Scientist* 63 (13):1810–1829.

Perkins, Anna Kasafi. 2011. "Carne vale (goodbye to flesh?): Caribbean carnival, notions of the flesh and Christian ambivalence about the body." *Sexuality & Culture* 15 (4):361–374.

Persadie, Ryan. 2021. "'Deh say I's ah madman': Soca performance, Afro-Caribbean masculinities, and the metaphorization of madness." *Caribbean Review of Gender Studies* (15):105–132.

Pertwee, E. 2020. "Donald Trump, the anti-Muslim far right and the new conservative revolution." *Ethnic and Racial Studies* 43 (16):211–230

Peterson, Russell Leslie. 2008. *Strange Bedfellows: How Late-Night Comedy Turns Democracy into a Joke:* Rutgers University Press.

Pickard, Victor. 2016. "Media and politics in the age of Trump." *Origins: Current Events in Historical Perspective* 10 (2).

Pickard, Victor. 2019. "The violence of the market." *Journalism* 20 (1):154–158.

Pirro, Andrea LP, and Paul Taggart. 2023. "Populists in power and conspiracy theories." *Party Politics* 29 (3):413–423.

Politico Staff. 2023. "Tracking the Trump criminal charges." *Politico*, August 16. https://www.politico.com/interactives/2023/trump-criminal-investigations-cases-tracker-list/.

Pomerantsev, Peter, and Michael Weiss. 2014. *The Menace of Unreality: How the Kremlin Weaponizes Information, Culture and Money:* Institute of Modern Russia.

Poniewozik, J, and M Lyons. 2017. "Matt Lauer, Charlie Rose and the Sexism of Morning TV." *The New York Times.* https://www.nytimes.com/2017/11/29/arts/television/matt-lauer-charlie-rose.html.

Poole, Elizabeth, Eva Haifa Giraud, and Ed de Quincey. 2021. "Tactical interventions in online hate speech: The case of #stopIslam." *New Media & Society* 23 (6):1415–1442. https://doi.org/10.1177/1461444820903319.

Popova, Irina. 2009. *Kniga MM Bakhtina o Fransua Rable i yeyo znacheniye dlya teorii literatury:* Federal'noye gosudarstvennoye byudzhetnoye uchrezhdeniye nauki Institut mirovoy literatury Ros. Akademii Nauk.

Porter, Laraine. 1998. "Tarts, tampons, and tyrants." In *Because I Tell a Joke or Two: Comedy, Politics, and Social Difference,* 65–93. Routledge.

Posner, Sarah, and David Neiwert. 2016. "How Trump took hate group mainstream: The full story of his connection with far-right extremists." MotherJones. Accessed November 7. https://www.motherjones.com/politics/2016/10/donald-trump-hate-groups-neo-nazi-white-supremacist-racism/.

Postman, Neil. 2006. *Amusing Ourselves to Death: Public Discourse in the Age of Show Business:* Penguin.

Purcell, Darren, Brooks Heitmeier, and Chad Van Wyhe. 2017. "Critical geopolitics and the framing of the Arab Spring through late-night humor." *Social Science Quarterly* 98 (2):513–531.

Quattrociocchi, Walter, Antonio Scala, and Cass R Sunstein. 2016. "Echo chambers on Facebook." Available at SSRN 2795110.

Rackaway, Chapman, and Laurie L Rice. 2018. *American Political Parties Under Pressure:* Palgrave Macmillan.

Ratkiewicz, J, M Conover, M Meiss, B Gonçalves, A Flammini, and F Menczer. 2011. "Detecting and tracking political abuse in social media." *Proceedings of the International AAAI Conference on Web and Social Media* 5 (1):297–304.

Ravenscroft, Neil, and Paul Gilchrist. 2009. "Spaces of transgression: Governance, discipline and reworking the carnivalesque." *Leisure Studies* 28 (1):35–49.

Rawnsley, Andrew. 2022. "One party after another: The disruptive life of Nigel Farage review—the man who broke Britain." *The Guardian,* February 6. https://www.theguardian.com/books/2022/feb/06/one-party-after-another-the-disruptive-life-of-nigel-farage-review-the-man-who-broke-britain.

Razack, Sabrina, and Janelle Joseph. 2021. "Misogynoir in women's sport media: Race, nation, and diaspora in the representation of Naomi Osaka." *Media, Culture & Society* 43 (2):291–308.

Regan, Helen. 2017. "Read the full transcript of President Trump's 2017 Boy Scout Jamboree speech." *TIME,* July 25. https://time.com/4872118/trump-boy-scout-jamboree-speech-transcript/.

Ritchie, Jessica. 2013. "Creating a monster: Online media constructions of Hillary Clinton during the democratic primary campaign, 2007–8." *Feminist Media Studies* 13 (1):102–119.

Roach, Joseph. 1995. "Culture and performance in the circum-Atlantic world." In *Performativity and Performance,* 45–63. Routledge.

Rogers, R. 2020. "Deplatforming: Following extreme Internet celebrities to Telegram and alternative social media." *European Journal of Communication* 35 (3):213–229.

Rogin, Michael. 1996. *Blackface, White Noise: Jewish Immigrants in the Hollywood Melting Pot:* University of California Press.

Roller, E. 2016. "Peter Thiel wants you to take Trump seriously, but not too seriously." *The New York Times*, November 1. http://www.nytimes.com/2016/11/01/opinion/campaign-stops/peter-thiel-wants-you-to-take-trump-seriously-but-not-too-seriously.html

Ronayne, Kathleen, and Michael Kunzelman. 2020. "Trump to far-right extremists: 'Stand back and stand by.'" *Associated Press*, September 30. https://apnews.com/article/election-2020-joe-biden-race-and-ethnicity-donald-trump-chris-wallace-0b32339da25fbc9e8b7c7c7066a1db0f

Rosa, Jonathan, and Yarimar Bonilla. 2017. "Deprovincializing Trump, decolonizing diversity, and unsettling anthropology." *American Ethnologist* 44 (2):201–208.

Rose, EM. 2015. *The Murder of William of Norwich: The Origins of the Blood Libel in Medieval Europe:* Oxford University Press.

Rowley, Alison. 2017. "'Trump and Putin sittin' in a tree': Material culture, slash and the pornographication of the 2016 US presidential election." *Porn Studies* 4 (4):381–405.

Rozsa, Matthew. 2016. "Donald Trump's last campaign ad is a fitting end to an anti-Semitic campaign." *Salon*, November 7. https://www.salon.com/2016/11/07/watch-donald-trumps-last-campaign-ad-is-a-fitting-end-to-an-anti-semitic-campaign/.

Rudwin, Maximilian J. 1919. "The origin of the German carnival comedy." *The Journal of English and Germanic Philology* 18 (3):402–454.

Russo, Mary. 1986. "Female grotesques: Carnival and theory." In *Feminist Studies/Critical Studies*, 213–229. Springer.

Saddik, Annette J. 2012. "'Drowned in Rabelaisian laughter': Germans as grotesque comic figures in the plays of Tennessee Williams." *Modern Drama* 55 (3):356–372.

Samoilenko, Sergei A, Eric Shiraev, Jennifer Keohane, and Martijn Icks. 2016. "Character assassination." In *The SAGE Encyclopedia of Corporate Reputation*, 1:115–118. Sage.

Saxton, Alexander. 1975. "Blackface minstrelsy and Jacksonian ideology." *American Quarterly* 27 (1):3–28.

Scher, Richard K. 2015. *The Politics of Disenfranchisement: Why Is It So Hard to Vote in America?:* Routledge.

Schlembach, Raphael. 2018. "Undercover policing and the spectre of 'domestic extremism': The covert surveillance of environmental activism in Britain." *Social Movement Studies* 17 (5):491–506.

Schmid, Julian. 2020. "(Captain) America in crisis: Popular digital culture and the negotiation of Americanness." *Cambridge Review of International Affairs* 33 (5):690–712.

Schmitt, Josephine B Diana Rieger, Olivia Rutkowski, Julian Ernst (2018) Counter-messages as Prevention or Promotion of Extremism?! The Potential Role of YouTube: Recommendation Algorithms, *Journal of Communication*, Volume 68, Issue 4, August 2018, Pages 780–808, https://doi.org/10.1093/joc/jqy029.

Schreckinger, Ben. 2017. "World war meme." *Politico Magazine*, March/April.

Schwarzenegger, Christian, and Anna JM Wagner. 2018. "Can it be hate if it is fun? Discursive ensembles of hatred and laughter in extreme right satire on Facebook." *Studies in Communication* 7 (4):473–498.

Sehmby, Dalbir S. 2002. "Wrestling and popular culture." *CLCWeb: Comparative Literature and Culture* 4 (1):5.

Serwer, A. 2018. "The cruelty is the point." *The Atlantic*, October 3. https://www.theatlantic.com/ideas/archive/2018/10/the-cruelty-is-the-point/572104/.

Serwer, A. 2021. *The Cruelty Is the Point: The Past, Present, and Future of Trump's America:* One World.

Shao, Guosong. 2009. "Understanding the appeal of user-generated media: A uses and gratification perspective." *Internet Research* 19 (1):7–25.

Shevtsova, Maria. 1992. "Dialogism in the novel and Bakhtin's theory of culture." *New Literary History* 23 (3):747–763.

Shklar, Judith N. 2013. "The liberalism of fear." In *Liberalism and the Moral Life*, 21–38. Harvard University Press.

Siapera, E., & Viejo-Otero, P. (2021). Governing Hate: Facebook and Digital Racism. *Television & New Media*, 22(2), 112–130. https://doi.org/10.1177/1527476420982232.

Sienkiewicz, Matt, and Nick Marx. 2022. *That's Not Funny: How the Right Makes Comedy Work for Them:* University of California Press.

Sindelar, Daisy. 2014. "The Kremlin's troll army." *The Atlantic* 12.

Smirnova, Michelle. 2018. "Small hands, nasty women, and bad hombres: Hegemonic masculinity and humor in the 2016 presidential election." *Socius* 4:2378023117749380.

Smith, Allan. 2020. "Bloomberg calls Trump a 'carnival barking clown' after president labels him a 'tiny version' of Jeb Bush." *NBC News*, February 13. https://www.nbcnews.com/politics/2020-election/trump-bloomberg-trade-blows-president-targets-democratic-contender-n1136296.

Smith, J Scott, and Sean Connable. 2021. "Minimizing the past and supporting the vessel: Evangelical leaders' third-party support for President Donald Trump during the Stormy Daniels scandal." *Journal of Communication & Religion* 44 (3):78–96.

Smith, Jamie Noelle. 2018. "No laughing matter: Failures of satire during the 2016 presidential election." University of New Hampshire.

Sobieraj, Sarah. 2018. "Bitch, slut, skank, cunt: Patterned resistance to women's visibility in digital publics." *Information, Communication & Society* 21 (11):1700–1714.

Sommerlad, Joe. 2019. "A short history of all the times Donald Trump has retweeted or engaged with white nationalist Twitter accounts." *indy100*, March 21. https://www.indy100.com/news/donald-trump-white-nationalism-neo-nazis-twitter-kkk-8830011.

Southern, Rosalynd, and Emily Harmer. 2019. "Othering political women: Online misogyny, racism and ableism towards women in public life." In *Online Othering*, 187–210. Springer.

Spackman, Barbara. 1996. *Fascist Virilities: Rhetoric, Ideology, and Social Fantasy in Italy:* University of Minnesota Press.

Spivak, Gayatri Chakravorty. 1999. *Can the Subaltern Speak?:* Harvard University Press.

Springhall, John. 2008. "Blackface minstrelsy: The first all-American show." In *The Genesis of Mass Culture: Show Business Live in America, 1840 to 1940*, 57–80. Springer.

Sprunt, Barbara. 2020 "The history behind 'When the looting starts, the shooting starts.'" *The NPR*, May 29. https://www.npr.org/2020/05/29/864818368/the-history-behind-when-the-looting-starts-the-shooting-starts.

Statt, N. (2020). "Facebook reportedly ignored its own research showing algorithms divided users". *The Verge*. 26 May 2020. https://www.theverge.com/2020/5/26/21270659/facebook-division-news-feed-algorithms.

Stevens, Adrian. 2007. "Carnival and comedy: On Bakhtin's misreading of Boccaccio." *Opticon1826* (3).

Stewart, Katherine, Talitha Dubow, Joanna Hofman, and Christian van Stolk. 2016. *Social Change and Public Engagement with Policy and Evidence*. RAND Corporation.

Streb, Matthew J, Barbara Burrell, Brian Frederick, and Michael A Genovese. 2008. "Social desirability effects and support for a female American president." *Public Opinion Quarterly* 72 (1):76–89.

Strolovitch, Dara Z, Janelle S Wong, and Andrew Proctor. 2017. "A possessive investment in white heteropatriarchy? The 2016 election and the politics of race, gender, and sexuality." *Politics, Groups, and Identities* 5 (2):353–363.

Strömbäck, Jesper. 2008. "Four phases of mediatization: An analysis of the mediatization of politics." *The International Journal of Press/Politics* 13 (3):228–246.

Sundén, Jenny, and Susanna Paasonen. 2018. "Shameless hags and tolerance whores: Feminist resistance and the affective circuits of online hate." *Feminist Media Studies* 18 (4):643–656.

Syvertsen, Trine. 2003. "Challenges to public television in the era of convergence and commercialization." *Television & New Media* 4 (2):155–175.

Taggart, Paul. 2002. "Populism and the pathology of representative politics." In *Democracies and the Populist Challenge*, 62–80. Springer.

Taylor, Jessica. 2015. "Trump calls for 'total and complete shutdown of Muslims entering' U.S." NPR, December 7. https://www.npr.org/2015/12/07/458836388/trump-calls-for-total-and-complete-shutdown-of-muslims-entering-u-s.

Taylor, Steven. 2018. "Grotesque leadership: The aesthetics of the 'mangled apricot hellbeast'." *Organizational Aesthetics* 7 (1):11–17.

Tesler, Michael. 2018. "Islamophobia in the 2016 election." *Journal of Race, Ethnicity, and Politics* 3 (1):153–155.

Thelwell, Chinua. 2020. *Exporting Jim Crow: Blackface Minstrelsy in South Africa and Beyond:* University of Massachusetts Press.

Theweleit, Klaus. 1987. *Male Fantasies: Women, Floods, Bodies, History.* Vol. 1: University of Minnesota Press.

Thomson, Philip. 2017. *The Grotesque:* Routledge.

Thorsen, Einar. 2018. "Afterword: Clinton, Trump, and artificial intelligence." In *Managing Democracy in the Digital Age*, 265–270. Springer.

Tobin, Robert Deam. 2017. "Gays for Trump? Homonationalism has deep roots." *The Gay & Lesbian Review Worldwide* 24 (3):5–8.

Topinka, Robert J. 2018. "Politically incorrect participatory media: Racist nationalism on r/ImGoingToHellForThis." *New Media & Society* 20 (5):2050–2069.

Truzzi, Marcello, and Patrick Easto. 1972. "Carnivals, road shows and freaks." *Society* 9 (5):26–34.

Tsakona, Villy, and D Popa. 2011. "Humour in politics and the politics of humour." In *Studies in Political Humour: In between Political Critique and Public Entertainment*, 1–30. John Benjamins.

Tsukamoto, Satoshi. 2002. "Hermeneutics of carnival and culture." *Language and Culture* 7:69–87.

Tunali, Tijen. 2018. "The art of resistance: Carnival aesthetics and the Gezi Street protests." *ASAP/Journal* 3 (2):377–399.

Twitchell, James B. 1993. *Carnival Culture: The Trashing of Taste in America:* Columbia University Press.

Tyler, Doctor Imogen. 2013. *Revolting Subjects: Social Abjection and Resistance in Neoliberal Britain:* Zed Books.

United States Office of the Director of National Intelligence. 2017. *Assessing Russian Activities and Intentions in Recent US Elections.*

Uscinski, Joseph E, and Lilly J Goren. 2011. "What's in a name? Coverage of senator Hillary Clinton during the 2008 democratic primary." *Political Research Quarterly* 64 (4):884–896.

Ussher, Jane M. 2013. "Diagnosing difficult women and pathologising femininity: Gender bias in psychiatric nosology." *Feminism & Psychology* 23 (1):63–69.

Van Dijck, José, and Thomas Poell. 2015. "Making public television social? Public service broadcasting and the challenges of social media." *Television & New Media* 16 (2):148–164.

Van Dijck, José, Thomas Poell, and Martijn de Waal. 2018. *The Platform Society: Public Values in a Connective World:* Oxford University Press.

Vidgen, Bertie, and Taha Yasseri. 2020. "Detecting weak and strong Islamophobic hate speech on social media." *Journal of Information Technology & Politics* 17 (1):66–78. https://doi.org/10.1080/19331681.2019.1702607.

Viladrich, Anahi. 2023. "'American tales of heroes and villains': Donald Trump's framing of Latinos during COVID-19 times." *Sociology of Race and Ethnicity.* https://doi.org/10.1177/23326492231177639.

Vitali, A, K Hunt, and F Thorp. 2018. "Trump referred to Haiti and African nations as 'shithole' countries." *NBC News*, January 11.

Wagner, Anna, and Christian Schwarzenegger. 2020. "A populism of lulz: The proliferation of humor, satire, and memes as populist communication in digital culture." In *Perspectives on Populism and the Media*, 313–332. Nomos.

Wahl-Jorgensen, Karin. 2019. "Media and the emotional politics of populism." In *Media and Populism*, 57–68. 1st Lisbon Winter School for the Study of Communication.

Waisanen, Don. 2019. "The political economy of late-night comedy." In *The Joke Is On Us: Political Comedy in (Late) Neoliberal Times*, 159–175. Lexington Books.

Wang, Yu, Yang Feng, Jiebo Luo, and Xiyang Zhang. 2016. "Pricing the woman card: Gender politics between Hillary Clinton and Donald Trump." 2016 IEEE International Conference on Big Data (Big Data).

Warner, Helen, and Heather Savigny. 2015. "'Where do you go after bridesmaids?': The politics of being a woman in Hollywood." In *The Politics of Being a Woman: Feminism, Media and 21st Century Popular Culture*, 112–131. Springer.

Webber, Julie, Mehnaaz Momen, Jessyka Finley, Rebecca Krefting, Cynthia Willett, and Julie Willett. 2021. "The political force of the comedic." *Contemporary Political Theory* 20:419–446.

Weeks, Brian E, and R Lance Holbert. 2013. "Predicting dissemination of news content in social media: A focus on reception, friending, and partisanship." *Journalism & Mass Communication Quarterly* 90 (2):212–232.

Weis, Diana. 2023. "Nazi-Barbies." In *The Cultural Politics of Anti-Elitism*, 243–260. Routledge.

Wells, Chris, Dhavan V Shah, Jon C Pevehouse, JungHwan Yang, Ayellet Pelled, Frederick Boehm, Josephine Lukito, Shreenita Ghosh, and Jessica L Schmidt. 2016. "How Trump drove coverage to the nomination: Hybrid media campaigning." *Political Communication* 33 (4):669–676.

Westfall, Jacob, Leaf Van Boven, John R Chambers, and Charles M Judd. 2015. "Perceiving political polarization in the United States party identity strength and attitude extremity exacerbate the perceived partisan divide." *Perspectives on Psychological Science* 10 (2):145–158.

White, Allon, and Peter Stallybrass. 1986. *The Politics and Poetics of Transgression:* Cornell University Press.

Whitehead, Andrew L, and Samuel L Perry. 2020. *Taking America Back for God: Christian Nationalism in the United States:* Oxford University Press.

Whittaker, J. & Looney, S. & Reed, A. & Votta, F. (2021). Recommender systems and the amplification of extremist content. Internet Policy Review, 10(2). https://doi.org/10.14763/2021.2.1565.

Wiedlack, Katharina. 2019. "In/visibly different: Melania Trump and the othering of Eastern European women in US culture." *Feminist Media Studies* 19 (8):1063–1078.

Williams, Michael C. 2003. "Words, images, enemies: Securitization and international politics." *International Studies Quarterly* 47 (4):511–531.

Winter, Aaron. 2019. "Online hate: From the far-right to the 'alt-right' and from the margins to the mainstream." In *Online Othering*, 39–63. Springer.

Wodak, Ruth. 2019. "Analysing the micropolitics of the populist far right in the 'post-shame era'." In *Europe at the Crossroads*, 63–92. Academic Press.

Wodak, Ruth. 2020. *The Politics of Fear: The Shameless Normalization of Far-Right Discourse:* Sage.

Wodak, Ruth, Jonathan Culpeper, and Elena Semino. 2021. "Shameless normalisation of impoliteness: Berlusconi's and Trump's press conferences." *Discourse & Society* 32 (3):369–393.

Wolfe, Michelle, Bryan D Jones, and Frank R Baumgartner. 2013. "A failure to communicate: Agenda setting in media and policy studies." *Political Communication* 30 (2):175–192.

Wood, Marcus. 2013. "Valency and abjection in the lynching postcard: A test case in the reclamation of black visual culture." *Slavery & Abolition* 34 (2):202–221.

Woods, Heather Suzanne, and Leslie A Hahner. 2019. *Make America Meme Again: The Rhetoric of the Alt-Right:* Peter Lang.

Wu, Anise MS, Vivi I Cheung, Lisbeth Ku, and Eva PW Hung. 2013. "Psychological risk factors of addiction to social networking sites among Chinese smartphone users." *Journal of Behavioral Addictions* 2 (3):160–166.

Yan, Grace, Ann Pegoraro, and Nicholas M Watanabe. 2019. "Examining IRA bots in the NFL anthem protest: Political agendas and practices of digital gatekeeping." *Communication & Sport:*2167479519849114.

Yates, Heather E. 2019. *The Politics of Spectacle and Emotion in the 2016 Presidential Campaign:* Springer.

Young, Dannagal Goldthwaite. 2019. *Irony and Outrage: The Polarized Landscape of Rage, Fear, and Laughter in the United States:* Oxford University Press.

Zadrozny, B. "'Carol's Journey': What Facebook knew about how it radicalized users". *NBC News.* 26 October 2021. https://www.nbcnews.com/tech/tech-news/facebook-knew-radicalized-users-rcna3581.

Zemon Davis, N. (1971). The Reasons of Misrule: Youth Groups and Charivaris in Sixteenth–Century France. *Past & Present,* 50(1), 41–75.

Zhao, Yuezhi. 1997. "Toward a propaganda/commercial model of journalism in China? The case of the Beijing Youth News." *Gazette (Leiden, Netherlands)* 58 (3):143–157.

Zito, S. 2016. "Taking Trump seriously, not literally." *The Atlantic*, September 23. http://www.theatlantic.com/politics/archive/2016/09/trump-makes-his-case-inpittsburgh/501335/.

Zittrain, J. 2014. "Engineering an election: Digital gerrymandering poses a threat to democracy." *Harvard Law Review* 127 (8):335–341.

Index

Note: We thank our student Sasha Padberg for her help in compiling the index.

www.ingramcontent.com/pod-product-compliance
Lightning Source LLC
Chambersburg PA
CBHW021623270326
41931CB00008B/846